CAREER EXAMINATION SERIES

MW00788165

THIS IS YOUR **PASSBOOK**® FOR ...

CHIEF WATER TREATMENT PLANT OPERATOR

NATIONAL LEARNING CORPORATION®
passbooks.com

PASSBOOK® SERIES

THE *PASSBOOK® SERIES* has been created to prepare applicants and candidates for the ultimate academic battlefield – the examination room.

At some time in our lives, each and every one of us may be required to take an examination – for validation, matriculation, admission, qualification, registration, certification, or licensure.

Based on the assumption that every applicant or candidate has met the basic formal educational standards, has taken the required number of courses, and read the necessary texts, the *PASSBOOK® SERIES* furnishes the one special preparation which may assure passing with confidence, instead of failing with insecurity. Examination questions – together with answers – are furnished as the basic vehicle for study so that the mysteries of the examination and its compounding difficulties may be eliminated or diminished by a sure method.

This book is meant to help you pass your examination provided that you qualify and are serious in your objective.

The entire field is reviewed through the huge store of content information which is succinctly presented through a provocative and challenging approach – the question-and-answer method.

A climate of success is established by furnishing the correct answers at the end of each test.

You soon learn to recognize types of questions, forms of questions, and patterns of questioning. You may even begin to anticipate expected outcomes.

You perceive that many questions are repeated or adapted so that you can gain acute insights, which may enable you to score many sure points.

You learn how to confront new questions, or types of questions, and to attack them confidently and work out the correct answers.

You note objectives and emphases, and recognize pitfalls and dangers, so that you may make positive educational adjustments.

Moreover, you are kept fully informed in relation to new concepts, methods, practices, and directions in the field.

You discover that you arre actually taking the examination all the time: you are preparing for the examination by "taking" an examination, not by reading extraneous and/or supererogatory textbooks.

In short, this PASSBOOK®, used directedly, should be an important factor in helping you to pass your test.

CHIEF WATER TREATMENT PLANT OPERATOR

DUTIES

Regulates flows into and out of the various pumping stations; makes necessary chemical and physical tests on water for proper treatment; records readings and adjusts equipment as required from interpretation of readings; makes and records chemical and physical tests on various treatment processes; performs other routine, operational, and maintenance tasks as required.

SCOPE OF THE WRITTEN TEST·

The written test will be designed to test for knowledge, skills, and/or abilities in such areas as:

1. Practices and equipment used in the operation and maintenance of a water treatment plant;
2. Principles and application of physics, chemistry and bacteriology as related to water treatment and purification;
3. Operation, maintenance, and repair of pumps, motors, valves, electrical and mechanical equipment; and
4. Supervision.

HOW TO TAKE A TEST

I. YOU MUST PASS AN EXAMINATION

A. WHAT EVERY CANDIDATE SHOULD KNOW

Examination applicants often ask us for help in preparing for the written test. What can I study in advance? What kinds of questions will be asked? How will the test be given? How will the papers be graded?

As an applicant for a civil service examination, you may be wondering about some of these things. Our purpose here is to suggest effective methods of advance study and to describe civil service examinations.

Your chances for success on this examination can be increased if you know how to prepare. Those "pre-examination jitters" can be reduced if you know what to expect. You can even experience an adventure in good citizenship if you know why civil service exams are given.

B. WHY ARE CIVIL SERVICE EXAMINATIONS GIVEN?

Civil service examinations are important to you in two ways. As a citizen, you want public jobs filled by employees who know how to do their work. As a job seeker, you want a fair chance to compete for that job on an equal footing with other candidates. The best-known means of accomplishing this two-fold goal is the competitive examination.

Exams are widely publicized throughout the nation. They may be administered for jobs in federal, state, city, municipal, town or village governments or agencies.

Any citizen may apply, with some limitations, such as the age or residence of applicants. Your experience and education may be reviewed to see whether you meet the requirements for the particular examination. When these requirements exist, they are reasonable and applied consistently to all applicants. Thus, a competitive examination may cause you some uneasiness now, but it is your privilege and safeguard.

C. HOW ARE CIVIL SERVICE EXAMS DEVELOPED?

Examinations are carefully written by trained technicians who are specialists in the field known as "psychological measurement," in consultation with recognized authorities in the field of work that the test will cover. These experts recommend the subject matter areas or skills to be tested; only those knowledges or skills important to your success on the job are included. The most reliable books and source materials available are used as references. Together, the experts and technicians judge the difficulty level of the questions.

Test technicians know how to phrase questions so that the problem is clearly stated. Their ethics do not permit "trick" or "catch" questions. Questions may have been tried out on sample groups, or subjected to statistical analysis, to determine their usefulness.

Written tests are often used in combination with performance tests, ratings of training and experience, and oral interviews. All of these measures combine to form the best-known means of finding the right person for the right job.

II. HOW TO PASS THE WRITTEN TEST

A. NATURE OF THE EXAMINATION

To prepare intelligently for civil service examinations, you should know how they differ from school examinations you have taken. In school you were assigned certain definite pages to read or subjects to cover. The examination questions were quite detailed and usually emphasized memory. Civil service exams, on the other hand, try to discover your present ability to perform the duties of a position, plus your potentiality to learn these duties. In other words, a civil service exam attempts to predict how successful you will be. Questions cover such a broad area that they cannot be as minute and detailed as school exam questions.

In the public service similar kinds of work, or positions, are grouped together in one "class." This process is known as *position-classification*. All the positions in a class are paid according to the salary range for that class. One class title covers all of these positions, and they are all tested by the same examination.

B. FOUR BASIC STEPS

1) Study the announcement

How, then, can you know what subjects to study? Our best answer is: "Learn as much as possible about the class of positions for which you've applied." The exam will test the knowledge, skills and abilities needed to do the work.

Your most valuable source of information about the position you want is the official exam announcement. This announcement lists the training and experience qualifications. Check these standards and apply only if you come reasonably close to meeting them.

The brief description of the position in the examination announcement offers some clues to the subjects which will be tested. Think about the job itself. Review the duties in your mind. Can you perform them, or are there some in which you are rusty? Fill in the blank spots in your preparation.

Many jurisdictions preview the written test in the exam announcement by including a section called "Knowledge and Abilities Required," "Scope of the Examination," or some similar heading. Here you will find out specifically what fields will be tested.

2) Review your own background

Once you learn in general what the position is all about, and what you need to know to do the work, ask yourself which subjects you already know fairly well and which need improvement. You may wonder whether to concentrate on improving your strong areas or on building some background in your fields of weakness. When the announcement has specified "some knowledge" or "considerable knowledge," or has used adjectives like "beginning principles of…" or "advanced … methods," you can get a clue as to the number and difficulty of questions to be asked in any given field. More questions, and hence broader coverage, would be included for those subjects which are more important in the work. Now weigh your strengths and weaknesses against the job requirements and prepare accordingly.

3) Determine the level of the position

Another way to tell how intensively you should prepare is to understand the level of the job for which you are applying. Is it the entering level? In other words, is this the position in which beginners in a field of work are hired? Or is it an intermediate or advanced level? Sometimes this is indicated by such words as "Junior" or "Senior" in the class title. Other jurisdictions use Roman numerals to designate the level – Clerk I, Clerk II, for example. The word "Supervisor" sometimes appears in the title. If the level is not indicated by the title, check the description of duties. Will you be working under very close supervision, or will you have responsibility for independent decisions in this work?

4) Choose appropriate study materials

Now that you know the subjects to be examined and the relative amount of each subject to be covered, you can choose suitable study materials. For beginning level jobs, or even advanced ones, if you have a pronounced weakness in some aspect of your training, read a modern, standard textbook in that field. Be sure it is up to date and has general coverage. Such books are normally available at your library, and the librarian will be glad to help you locate one. For entry-level positions, questions of appropriate difficulty are chosen – neither highly advanced questions, nor those too simple. Such questions require careful thought but not advanced training.

If the position for which you are applying is technical or advanced, you will read more advanced, specialized material. If you are already familiar with the basic principles of your field, elementary textbooks would waste your time. Concentrate on advanced textbooks and technical periodicals. Think through the concepts and review difficult problems in your field.

These are all general sources. You can get more ideas on your own initiative, following these leads. For example, training manuals and publications of the government agency which employs workers in your field can be useful, particularly for technical and professional positions. A letter or visit to the government department involved may result in more specific study suggestions, and certainly will provide you with a more definite idea of the exact nature of the position you are seeking.

III. KINDS OF TESTS

Tests are used for purposes other than measuring knowledge and ability to perform specified duties. For some positions, it is equally important to test ability to make adjustments to new situations or to profit from training. In others, basic mental abilities not dependent on information are essential. Questions which test these things may not appear as pertinent to the duties of the position as those which test for knowledge and information. Yet they are often highly important parts of a fair examination. For very general questions, it is almost impossible to help you direct your study efforts. What we can do is to point out some of the more common of these general abilities needed in public service positions and describe some typical questions.

1) General information

Broad, general information has been found useful for predicting job success in some kinds of work. This is tested in a variety of ways, from vocabulary lists to questions about current events. Basic background in some field of work, such as sociology or economics, may be sampled in a group of questions. Often these are principles which have become familiar to most persons through exposure rather than through formal training. It is difficult to advise you how to study for these questions; being alert to the world around you is our best suggestion.

2) Verbal ability

An example of an ability needed in many positions is verbal or language ability. Verbal ability is, in brief, the ability to use and understand words. Vocabulary and grammar tests are typical measures of this ability. Reading comprehension or paragraph interpretation questions are common in many kinds of civil service tests. You are given a paragraph of written material and asked to find its central meaning.

3) Numerical ability

Number skills can be tested by the familiar arithmetic problem, by checking paired lists of numbers to see which are alike and which are different, or by interpreting charts and graphs. In the latter test, a graph may be printed in the test booklet which you are asked to use as the basis for answering questions.

4) Observation

A popular test for law-enforcement positions is the observation test. A picture is shown to you for several minutes, then taken away. Questions about the picture test your ability to observe both details and larger elements.

5) Following directions

In many positions in the public service, the employee must be able to carry out written instructions dependably and accurately. You may be given a chart with several columns, each column listing a variety of information. The questions require you to carry out directions involving the information given in the chart.

6) Skills and aptitudes

Performance tests effectively measure some manual skills and aptitudes. When the skill is one in which you are trained, such as typing or shorthand, you can practice. These tests are often very much like those given in business school or high school courses. For many of the other skills and aptitudes, however, no short-time preparation can be made. Skills and abilities natural to you or that you have developed throughout your lifetime are being tested.

Many of the general questions just described provide all the data needed to answer the questions and ask you to use your reasoning ability to find the answers. Your best preparation for these tests, as well as for tests of facts and ideas, is to be at your physical and mental best. You, no doubt, have your own methods of getting into an exam-taking mood and keeping "in shape." The next section lists some ideas on this subject.

IV. KINDS OF QUESTIONS

Only rarely is the "essay" question, which you answer in narrative form, used in civil service tests. Civil service tests are usually of the short-answer type. Full instructions for answering these questions will be given to you at the examination. But in case this is your first experience with short-answer questions and separate answer sheets, here is what you need to know:

1) Multiple-choice Questions

Most popular of the short-answer questions is the "multiple choice" or "best answer" question. It can be used, for example, to test for factual knowledge, ability to solve problems or judgment in meeting situations found at work.

A multiple-choice question is normally one of three types—

- It can begin with an incomplete statement followed by several possible endings. You are to find the one ending which *best* completes the statement, although some of the others may not be entirely wrong.
- It can also be a complete statement in the form of a question which is answered by choosing one of the statements listed.
- It can be in the form of a problem – again you select the best answer.

Here is an example of a multiple-choice question with a discussion which should give you some clues as to the method for choosing the right answer:

When an employee has a complaint about his assignment, the action which will *best* help him overcome his difficulty is to
- A. discuss his difficulty with his coworkers
- B. take the problem to the head of the organization
- C. take the problem to the person who gave him the assignment
- D. say nothing to anyone about his complaint

In answering this question, you should study each of the choices to find which is best. Consider choice "A" – Certainly an employee may discuss his complaint with fellow employees, but no change or improvement can result, and the complaint remains unresolved. Choice "B" is a poor choice since the head of the organization probably does not know what assignment you have been given, and taking your problem to him is known as "going over the head" of the supervisor. The supervisor, or person who made the assignment, is the person who can clarify it or correct any injustice. Choice "C" is, therefore, correct. To say nothing, as in choice "D," is unwise. Supervisors have and interest in knowing the problems employees are facing, and the employee is seeking a solution to his problem.

2) True/False Questions

The "true/false" or "right/wrong" form of question is sometimes used. Here a complete statement is given. Your job is to decide whether the statement is right or wrong.

SAMPLE: A roaming cell-phone call to a nearby city costs less than a non-roaming call to a distant city.

This statement is wrong, or false, since roaming calls are more expensive.

This is not a complete list of all possible question forms, although most of the others are variations of these common types. You will always get complete directions for answering questions. Be sure you understand *how* to mark your answers – ask questions until you do.

V. RECORDING YOUR ANSWERS

Computer terminals are used more and more today for many different kinds of exams.

For an examination with very few applicants, you may be told to record your answers in the test booklet itself. Separate answer sheets are much more common. If this separate answer sheet is to be scored by machine – and this is often the case – it is highly important that you mark your answers correctly in order to get credit.

An electronic scoring machine is often used in civil service offices because of the speed with which papers can be scored. Machine-scored answer sheets must be marked with a pencil, which will be given to you. This pencil has a high graphite content which responds to the electronic scoring machine. As a matter of fact, stray dots may register as answers, so do not let your pencil rest on the answer sheet while you are pondering the correct answer. Also, if your pencil lead breaks or is otherwise defective, ask for another.

Since the answer sheet will be dropped in a slot in the scoring machine, be careful not to bend the corners or get the paper crumpled.

The answer sheet normally has five vertical columns of numbers, with 30 numbers to a column. These numbers correspond to the question numbers in your test booklet. After each number, going across the page are four or five pairs of dotted lines. These short dotted lines have small letters or numbers above them. The first two pairs may also have a "T" or "F" above the letters. This indicates that the first two pairs only are to be used if the questions are of the true-false type. If the questions are multiple choice, disregard the "T" and "F" and pay attention only to the small letters or numbers.

Answer your questions in the manner of the sample that follows:

32. The largest city in the United States is
    A. Washington, D.C.
    B. New York City
    C. Chicago
    D. Detroit
    E. San Francisco

1) Choose the answer you think is best. (New York City is the largest, so "B" is correct.)
2) Find the row of dotted lines numbered the same as the question you are answering. (Find row number 32)
3) Find the pair of dotted lines corresponding to the answer. (Find the pair of lines under the mark "B.")
4) Make a solid black mark between the dotted lines.

VI. BEFORE THE TEST

Common sense will help you find procedures to follow to get ready for an examination. Too many of us, however, overlook these sensible measures. Indeed, nervousness and fatigue have been found to be the most serious reasons why applicants fail to do their best on civil service tests. Here is a list of reminders:

- Begin your preparation early – Don't wait until the last minute to go scurrying around for books and materials or to find out what the position is all about.
- Prepare continuously – An hour a night for a week is better than an all-night cram session. This has been definitely established. What is more, a night a week for a month will return better dividends than crowding your study into a shorter period of time.
- Locate the place of the exam – You have been sent a notice telling you when and where to report for the examination. If the location is in a different town or otherwise unfamiliar to you, it would be well to inquire the best route and learn something about the building.
- Relax the night before the test – Allow your mind to rest. Do not study at all that night. Plan some mild recreation or diversion; then go to bed early and get a good night's sleep.
- Get up early enough to make a leisurely trip to the place for the test – This way unforeseen events, traffic snarls, unfamiliar buildings, etc. will not upset you.
- Dress comfortably – A written test is not a fashion show. You will be known by number and not by name, so wear something comfortable.
- Leave excess paraphernalia at home – Shopping bags and odd bundles will get in your way. You need bring only the items mentioned in the official notice you received; usually everything you need is provided. Do not bring reference books to the exam. They will only confuse those last minutes and be taken away from you when in the test room.
- Arrive somewhat ahead of time – If because of transportation schedules you must get there very early, bring a newspaper or magazine to take your mind off yourself while waiting.
- Locate the examination room – When you have found the proper room, you will be directed to the seat or part of the room where you will sit. Sometimes you are given a sheet of instructions to read while you are waiting. Do not fill out any forms until you are told to do so; just read them and be prepared.
- Relax and prepare to listen to the instructions
- If you have any physical problem that may keep you from doing your best, be sure to tell the test administrator. If you are sick or in poor health, you really cannot do your best on the exam. You can come back and take the test some other time.

VII. AT THE TEST

The day of the test is here and you have the test booklet in your hand. The temptation to get going is very strong. Caution! There is more to success than knowing the right answers. You must know how to identify your papers and understand variations in the type of short-answer question used in this particular examination. Follow these suggestions for maximum results from your efforts:

1) Cooperate with the monitor

The test administrator has a duty to create a situation in which you can be as much at ease as possible. He will give instructions, tell you when to begin, check to see that you are marking your answer sheet correctly, and so on. He is not there to guard you, although he will see that your competitors do not take unfair advantage. He wants to help you do your best.

2) Listen to all instructions

Don't jump the gun! Wait until you understand all directions. In most civil service tests you get more time than you need to answer the questions. So don't be in a hurry. Read each word of instructions until you clearly understand the meaning. Study the examples, listen to all announcements and follow directions. Ask questions if you do not understand what to do.

3) Identify your papers

Civil service exams are usually identified by number only. You will be assigned a number; you must not put your name on your test papers. Be sure to copy your number correctly. Since more than one exam may be given, copy your exact examination title.

4) Plan your time

Unless you are told that a test is a "speed" or "rate of work" test, speed itself is usually not important. Time enough to answer all the questions will be provided, but this does not mean that you have all day. An overall time limit has been set. Divide the total time (in minutes) by the number of questions to determine the approximate time you have for each question.

5) Do not linger over difficult questions

If you come across a difficult question, mark it with a paper clip (useful to have along) and come back to it when you have been through the booklet. One caution if you do this – be sure to skip a number on your answer sheet as well. Check often to be sure that you have not lost your place and that you are marking in the row numbered the same as the question you are answering.

6) Read the questions

Be sure you know what the question asks! Many capable people are unsuccessful because they failed to *read* the questions correctly.

7) Answer all questions

Unless you have been instructed that a penalty will be deducted for incorrect answers, it is better to guess than to omit a question.

8) Speed tests

It is often better NOT to guess on speed tests. It has been found that on timed tests people are tempted to spend the last few seconds before time is called in marking answers at random – without even reading them – in the hope of picking up a few extra points. To discourage this practice, the instructions may warn you that your score will be "corrected" for guessing. That is, a penalty will be applied. The incorrect answers will be deducted from the correct ones, or some other penalty formula will be used.

9) Review your answers

      If you finish before time is called, go back to the questions you guessed or omitted to give them further thought. Review other answers if you have time.

10) Return your test materials

      If you are ready to leave before others have finished or time is called, take ALL your materials to the monitor and leave quietly. Never take any test material with you. The monitor can discover whose papers are not complete, and taking a test booklet may be grounds for disqualification.

VIII. EXAMINATION TECHNIQUES

1) Read the general instructions carefully. These are usually printed on the first page of the exam booklet. As a rule, these instructions refer to the timing of the examination; the fact that you should not start work until the signal and must stop work at a signal, etc. If there are any *special* instructions, such as a choice of questions to be answered, make sure that you note this instruction carefully.

2) When you are ready to start work on the examination, that is as soon as the signal has been given, read the instructions to each question booklet, underline any key words or phrases, such as *least, best, outline, describe* and the like. In this way you will tend to answer as requested rather than discover on reviewing your paper that you *listed without describing*, that you selected the *worst* choice rather than the *best* choice, etc.

3) If the examination is of the objective or multiple-choice type – that is, each question will also give a series of possible answers: A, B, C or D, and you are called upon to select the best answer and write the letter next to that answer on your answer paper – it is advisable to start answering each question in turn. There may be anywhere from 50 to 100 such questions in the three or four hours allotted and you can see how much time would be taken if you read through all the questions before beginning to answer any. Furthermore, if you come across a question or group of questions which you know would be difficult to answer, it would undoubtedly affect your handling of all the other questions.

4) If the examination is of the essay type and contains but a few questions, it is a moot point as to whether you should read all the questions before starting to answer any one. Of course, if you are given a choice – say five out of seven and the like – then it is essential to read all the questions so you can eliminate the two that are most difficult. If, however, you are asked to answer all the questions, there may be danger in trying to answer the easiest one first because you may find that you will spend too much time on it. The best technique is to answer the first question, then proceed to the second, etc.

5) Time your answers. Before the exam begins, write down the time it started, then add the time allowed for the examination and write down the time it must be completed, then divide the time available somewhat as follows:

- If 3-1/2 hours are allowed, that would be 210 minutes. If you have 80 objective-type questions, that would be an average of 2-1/2 minutes per question. Allow yourself no more than 2 minutes per question, or a total of 160 minutes, which will permit about 50 minutes to review.
- If for the time allotment of 210 minutes there are 7 essay questions to answer, that would average about 30 minutes a question. Give yourself only 25 minutes per question so that you have about 35 minutes to review.

6) The most important instruction is to *read each question* and make sure you know what is wanted. The second most important instruction is to *time yourself properly* so that you answer every question. The third most important instruction is to *answer every question*. Guess if you have to but include something for each question. Remember that you will receive no credit for a blank and will probably receive some credit if you write something in answer to an essay question. If you guess a letter – say "B" for a multiple-choice question – you may have guessed right. If you leave a blank as an answer to a multiple-choice question, the examiners may respect your feelings but it will not add a point to your score. Some exams may penalize you for wrong answers, so in such cases *only*, you may not want to guess unless you have some basis for your answer.

7) Suggestions
   a. Objective-type questions
      1. Examine the question booklet for proper sequence of pages and questions
      2. Read all instructions carefully
      3. Skip any question which seems too difficult; return to it after all other questions have been answered
      4. Apportion your time properly; do not spend too much time on any single question or group of questions
      5. Note and underline key words – *all, most, fewest, least, best, worst, same, opposite,* etc.
      6. Pay particular attention to negatives
      7. Note unusual option, e.g., unduly long, short, complex, different or similar in content to the body of the question
      8. Observe the use of "hedging" words – *probably, may, most likely,* etc.
      9. Make sure that your answer is put next to the same number as the question
      10. Do not second-guess unless you have good reason to believe the second answer is definitely more correct
      11. Cross out original answer if you decide another answer is more accurate; do not erase until you are ready to hand your paper in
      12. Answer all questions; guess unless instructed otherwise
      13. Leave time for review

   b. Essay questions
      1. Read each question carefully
      2. Determine exactly what is wanted. Underline key words or phrases.
      3. Decide on outline or paragraph answer

4. Include many different points and elements unless asked to develop any one or two points or elements
5. Show impartiality by giving pros and cons unless directed to select one side only
6. Make and write down any assumptions you find necessary to answer the questions
7. Watch your English, grammar, punctuation and choice of words
8. Time your answers; don't crowd material

8) Answering the essay question

Most essay questions can be answered by framing the specific response around several key words or ideas. Here are a few such key words or ideas:

M's: manpower, materials, methods, money, management
P's: purpose, program, policy, plan, procedure, practice, problems, pitfalls, personnel, public relations
   a. Six basic steps in handling problems:
      1. Preliminary plan and background development
      2. Collect information, data and facts
      3. Analyze and interpret information, data and facts
      4. Analyze and develop solutions as well as make recommendations
      5. Prepare report and sell recommendations
      6. Install recommendations and follow up effectiveness

   b. Pitfalls to avoid
      1. *Taking things for granted* – A statement of the situation does not necessarily imply that each of the elements is necessarily true; for example, a complaint may be invalid and biased so that all that can be taken for granted is that a complaint has been registered
      2. *Considering only one side of a situation* – Wherever possible, indicate several alternatives and then point out the reasons you selected the best one
      3. *Failing to indicate follow up* – Whenever your answer indicates action on your part, make certain that you will take proper follow-up action to see how successful your recommendations, procedures or actions turn out to be
      4. *Taking too long in answering any single question* – Remember to time your answers properly

IX. AFTER THE TEST

Scoring procedures differ in detail among civil service jurisdictions although the general principles are the same. Whether the papers are hand-scored or graded by machine we have described, they are nearly always graded by number. That is, the person who marks the paper knows only the number – never the name – of the applicant. Not until all the papers have been graded will they be matched with names. If other tests, such as training and experience or oral interview ratings have been given, scores will be combined. Different parts of the examination usually have different weights. For example, the written test might count 60 percent of the final grade, and a rating of training and experience 40 percent. In many jurisdictions, veterans will have a certain number of points added to their grades.

After the final grade has been determined, the names are placed in grade order and an eligible list is established. There are various methods for resolving ties between those who get the same final grade – probably the most common is to place first the name of the person whose application was received first. Job offers are made from the eligible list in the order the names appear on it. You will be notified of your grade and your rank as soon as all these computations have been made. This will be done as rapidly as possible.

People who are found to meet the requirements in the announcement are called "eligibles." Their names are put on a list of eligible candidates. An eligible's chances of getting a job depend on how high he stands on this list and how fast agencies are filling jobs from the list.

When a job is to be filled from a list of eligibles, the agency asks for the names of people on the list of eligibles for that job. When the civil service commission receives this request, it sends to the agency the names of the three people highest on this list. Or, if the job to be filled has specialized requirements, the office sends the agency the names of the top three persons who meet these requirements from the general list.

The appointing officer makes a choice from among the three people whose names were sent to him. If the selected person accepts the appointment, the names of the others are put back on the list to be considered for future openings.

That is the rule in hiring from all kinds of eligible lists, whether they are for typist, carpenter, chemist, or something else. For every vacancy, the appointing officer has his choice of any one of the top three eligibles on the list. This explains why the person whose name is on top of the list sometimes does not get an appointment when some of the persons lower on the list do. If the appointing officer chooses the second or third eligible, the No. 1 eligible does not get a job at once, but stays on the list until he is appointed or the list is terminated.

X. HOW TO PASS THE INTERVIEW TEST

The examination for which you applied requires an oral interview test. You have already taken the written test and you are now being called for the interview test – the final part of the formal examination.

You may think that it is not possible to prepare for an interview test and that there are no procedures to follow during an interview. Our purpose is to point out some things you can do in advance that will help you and some good rules to follow and pitfalls to avoid while you are being interviewed.

What is an interview supposed to test?
The written examination is designed to test the technical knowledge and competence of the candidate; the oral is designed to evaluate intangible qualities, not readily measured otherwise, and to establish a list showing the relative fitness of each candidate – as measured against his competitors – for the position sought. Scoring is not on the basis of "right" and "wrong," but on a sliding scale of values ranging from "not passable" to "outstanding." As a matter of fact, it is possible to achieve a relatively low score without a single "incorrect" answer because of evident weakness in the qualities being measured.

Occasionally, an examination may consist entirely of an oral test – either an individual or a group oral. In such cases, information is sought concerning the technical knowledges and abilities of the candidate, since there has been no written examination for this purpose. More commonly, however, an oral test is used to supplement a written examination.

Who conducts interviews?

The composition of oral boards varies among different jurisdictions. In nearly all, a representative of the personnel department serves as chairman. One of the members of the board may be a representative of the department in which the candidate would work. In some cases, "outside experts" are used, and, frequently, a businessman or some other representative of the general public is asked to serve. Labor and management or other special groups may be represented. The aim is to secure the services of experts in the appropriate field.

However the board is composed, it is a good idea (and not at all improper or unethical) to ascertain in advance of the interview who the members are and what groups they represent. When you are introduced to them, you will have some idea of their backgrounds and interests, and at least you will not stutter and stammer over their names.

What should be done before the interview?

While knowledge about the board members is useful and takes some of the surprise element out of the interview, there is other preparation which is more substantive. It *is* possible to prepare for an oral interview – in several ways:

1) Keep a copy of your application and review it carefully before the interview

This may be the only document before the oral board, and the starting point of the interview. Know what education and experience you have listed there, and the sequence and dates of all of it. Sometimes the board will ask you to review the highlights of your experience for them; you should not have to hem and haw doing it.

2) Study the class specification and the examination announcement

Usually, the oral board has one or both of these to guide them. The qualities, characteristics or knowledges required by the position sought are stated in these documents. They offer valuable clues as to the nature of the oral interview. For example, if the job involves supervisory responsibilities, the announcement will usually indicate that knowledge of modern supervisory methods and the qualifications of the candidate as a supervisor will be tested. If so, you can expect such questions, frequently in the form of a hypothetical situation which you are expected to solve. NEVER go into an oral without knowledge of the duties and responsibilities of the job you seek.

3) Think through each qualification required

Try to visualize the kind of questions you would ask if you were a board member. How well could you answer them? Try especially to appraise your own knowledge and background in each area, *measured against the job sought*, and identify any areas in which you are weak. Be critical and realistic – do not flatter yourself.

4) Do some general reading in areas in which you feel you may be weak

For example, if the job involves supervision and your past experience has NOT, some general reading in supervisory methods and practices, particularly in the field of human relations, might be useful. Do NOT study agency procedures or detailed manuals. The oral board will be testing your understanding and capacity, not your memory.

5) Get a good night's sleep and watch your general health and mental attitude

You will want a clear head at the interview. Take care of a cold or any other minor ailment, and of course, no hangovers.

What should be done on the day of the interview?

Now comes the day of the interview itself. Give yourself plenty of time to get there. Plan to arrive somewhat ahead of the scheduled time, particularly if your appointment is in the fore part of the day. If a previous candidate fails to appear, the board might be ready for you a bit early. By early afternoon an oral board is almost invariably behind schedule if there are many candidates, and you may have to wait. Take along a book or magazine to read, or your application to review, but leave any extraneous material in the waiting room when you go in for your interview. In any event, relax and compose yourself.

The matter of dress is important. The board is forming impressions about you – from your experience, your manners, your attitude, and your appearance. Give your personal appearance careful attention. Dress your best, but not your flashiest. Choose conservative, appropriate clothing, and be sure it is immaculate. This is a business interview, and your appearance should indicate that you regard it as such. Besides, being well groomed and properly dressed will help boost your confidence.

Sooner or later, someone will call your name and escort you into the interview room. *This is it.* From here on you are on your own. It is too late for any more preparation. But remember, you asked for this opportunity to prove your fitness, and you are here because your request was granted.

What happens when you go in?

The usual sequence of events will be as follows: The clerk (who is often the board stenographer) will introduce you to the chairman of the oral board, who will introduce you to the other members of the board. Acknowledge the introductions before you sit down. Do not be surprised if you find a microphone facing you or a stenotypist sitting by. Oral interviews are usually recorded in the event of an appeal or other review.

Usually the chairman of the board will open the interview by reviewing the highlights of your education and work experience from your application – primarily for the benefit of the other members of the board, as well as to get the material into the record. Do not interrupt or comment unless there is an error or significant misinterpretation; if that is the case, do not hesitate. But do not quibble about insignificant matters. Also, he will usually ask you some question about your education, experience or your present job – partly to get you to start talking and to establish the interviewing "rapport." He may start the actual questioning, or turn it over to one of the other members. Frequently, each member undertakes the questioning on a particular area, one in which he is perhaps most competent, so you can expect each member to participate in the examination. Because time is limited, you may also expect some rather abrupt switches in the direction the questioning takes, so do not be upset by it. Normally, a board member will not pursue a single line of questioning unless he discovers a particular strength or weakness.

After each member has participated, the chairman will usually ask whether any member has any further questions, then will ask you if you have anything you wish to add. Unless you are expecting this question, it may floor you. Worse, it may start you off on an extended, extemporaneous speech. The board is not usually seeking more information. The question is principally to offer you a last opportunity to present further qualifications or to indicate that you have nothing to add. So, if you feel that a significant qualification or characteristic has been overlooked, it is proper to point it out in a sentence or so. Do not compliment the board on the thoroughness of their examination – they have been sketchy, and you know it. If you wish, merely say, "No thank you, I have nothing further to add." This is a point where you can "talk yourself out" of a good impression or fail to present an important bit of information. Remember, *you close the interview yourself.*

The chairman will then say, "That is all, Mr. _____, thank you." Do not be startled; the interview is over, and quicker than you think. Thank him, gather your belongings and take your leave. Save your sigh of relief for the other side of the door.

How to put your best foot forward
Throughout this entire process, you may feel that the board individually and collectively is trying to pierce your defenses, seek out your hidden weaknesses and embarrass and confuse you. Actually, this is not true. They are obliged to make an appraisal of your qualifications for the job you are seeking, and they want to see you in your best light. Remember, they must interview all candidates and a non-cooperative candidate may become a failure in spite of their best efforts to bring out his qualifications. Here are 15 suggestions that will help you:

1) Be natural – Keep your attitude confident, not cocky
If you are not confident that you can do the job, do not expect the board to be. Do not apologize for your weaknesses, try to bring out your strong points. The board is interested in a positive, not negative, presentation. Cockiness will antagonize any board member and make him wonder if you are covering up a weakness by a false show of strength.

2) Get comfortable, but don't lounge or sprawl
Sit erectly but not stiffly. A careless posture may lead the board to conclude that you are careless in other things, or at least that you are not impressed by the importance of the occasion. Either conclusion is natural, even if incorrect. Do not fuss with your clothing, a pencil or an ashtray. Your hands may occasionally be useful to emphasize a point; do not let them become a point of distraction.

3) Do not wisecrack or make small talk
This is a serious situation, and your attitude should show that you consider it as such. Further, the time of the board is limited – they do not want to waste it, and neither should you.

4) Do not exaggerate your experience or abilities
In the first place, from information in the application or other interviews and sources, the board may know more about you than you think. Secondly, you probably will not get away with it. An experienced board is rather adept at spotting such a situation, so do not take the chance.

5) If you know a board member, do not make a point of it, yet do not hide it

Certainly you are not fooling him, and probably not the other members of the board. Do not try to take advantage of your acquaintanceship – it will probably do you little good.

6) Do not dominate the interview

Let the board do that. They will give you the clues – do not assume that you have to do all the talking. Realize that the board has a number of questions to ask you, and do not try to take up all the interview time by showing off your extensive knowledge of the answer to the first one.

7) Be attentive

You only have 20 minutes or so, and you should keep your attention at its sharpest throughout. When a member is addressing a problem or question to you, give him your undivided attention. Address your reply principally to him, but do not exclude the other board members.

8) Do not interrupt

A board member may be stating a problem for you to analyze. He will ask you a question when the time comes. Let him state the problem, and wait for the question.

9) Make sure you understand the question

Do not try to answer until you are sure what the question is. If it is not clear, restate it in your own words or ask the board member to clarify it for you. However, do not haggle about minor elements.

10) Reply promptly but not hastily

A common entry on oral board rating sheets is "candidate responded readily," or "candidate hesitated in replies." Respond as promptly and quickly as you can, but do not jump to a hasty, ill-considered answer.

11) Do not be peremptory in your answers

A brief answer is proper – but do not fire your answer back. That is a losing game from your point of view. The board member can probably ask questions much faster than you can answer them.

12) Do not try to create the answer you think the board member wants

He is interested in what kind of mind you have and how it works – not in playing games. Furthermore, he can usually spot this practice and will actually grade you down on it.

13) Do not switch sides in your reply merely to agree with a board member

Frequently, a member will take a contrary position merely to draw you out and to see if you are willing and able to defend your point of view. Do not start a debate, yet do not surrender a good position. If a position is worth taking, it is worth defending.

14) Do not be afraid to admit an error in judgment if you are shown to be wrong

The board knows that you are forced to reply without any opportunity for careful consideration. Your answer may be demonstrably wrong. If so, admit it and get on with the interview.

15) Do not dwell at length on your present job

The opening question may relate to your present assignment. Answer the question but do not go into an extended discussion. You are being examined for a *new* job, not your present one. As a matter of fact, try to phrase ALL your answers in terms of the job for which you are being examined.

Basis of Rating

Probably you will forget most of these "do's" and "don'ts" when you walk into the oral interview room. Even remembering them all will not ensure you a passing grade. Perhaps you did not have the qualifications in the first place. But remembering them will help you to put your best foot forward, without treading on the toes of the board members.

Rumor and popular opinion to the contrary notwithstanding, an oral board wants you to make the best appearance possible. They know you are under pressure – but they also want to see how you respond to it as a guide to what your reaction would be under the pressures of the job you seek. They will be influenced by the degree of poise you display, the personal traits you show and the manner in which you respond.

ABOUT THIS BOOK

This book contains tests divided into Examination Sections. Go through each test, answering every question in the margin. At the end of each test look at the answer key and check your answers. On the ones you got wrong, look at the right answer choice and learn. Do not fill in the answers first. Do not memorize the questions and answers, but understand the answer and principles involved. On your test, the questions will likely be different from the samples. Questions are changed and new ones added. If you understand these past questions you should have success with any changes that arise. Tests may consist of several types of questions. We have additional books on each subject should more study be advisable or necessary for you. Finally, the more you study, the better prepared you will be. This book is intended to be the last thing you study before you walk into the examination room. Prior study of relevant texts is also recommended. NLC publishes some of these in our Fundamental Series. Knowledge and good sense are important factors in passing your exam. Good luck also helps. So now study this Passbook, absorb the material contained within and take that knowledge into the examination. Then do your best to pass that exam.

EXAMINATION SECTION

EXAMINATION SECTION
TEST 1

DIRECTIONS: Each question or incomplete statement is followed by several suggested answers or completions. Select the one the BEST answers the question or completes the statement. *PRINT THE LETTER OF THE CORRECT ANSWER IN THE SPACE AT THE RIGHT.*

1. Potential contaminants of drinking water as a consequence of disinfection treatment include each of the following, EXCEPT   1.____

    A. Hypochlorous acid
    B. Chlorite
    C. Chlorine dioxide
    D. Chloramine

2. Substances applied in the pretreatment of raw water that has undergone eutrophication typically include   2.____
     I.   Sodium phosphate
     II. Sodium thiosulphate
     III. Chlorine
     IV. Copper sulfate

    A. I and II
    B. II and III
    C. III and IV
    D. I, II, III and IV

3. Which of the following processes typically occurs EARLIEST in the water treatment sequence?   3.____

    A. Direct filtration
    B. Fluoridation
    C. Chlorination
    D. Disinfection

4. The major inconvenience of prolonged pre-treatment storage in an artificial tank or reservoir is   4.____

    A. excessive turbidity
    B. eutrophication
    C. the accumulation of sludge
    D. the loss of dissolved oxygen

5. The large majority of public water systems will register a pH that is   5.____

    A. absolutely neutral
    B. slightly basic
    C. slightly acid
    D. moderately acid

6. The most reliable absorber of synthetic organic chemicals in water is   6.____

     A. sodium thiosulfate
     B. activated carbon
     C. silica gel
     D. activated alumina

7. Which of the following contaminants is classified as a primary drinking water standard by the EPA?   7.____

     A. Coliform group
     B. Foaming agents
     C. Total dissolved solids
     D. Corrosivity

8. Typically, the temperature of water sampled for an Odor Threshold Test should be between _____ ° C.   8.____

     A. 10-15
     B. 25-40
     C. 40-60
     D. 65-85

9. Which of the following types of water analyses requires the largest sample volume?   9.____

     A. Biological oxygen demand (BOD)
     B. pH
     C. Chlorine
     D. Total solids

10. A _____ solution of an acid is one that contains 1.008 gram of replaceable hydrogen in one liter of solution.   10.____

     A. saturated
     B. molar
     C. supersaturated
     D. normal

11. Which of the following chemicals has been assigned a maximum contaminant level (MCL) by the EPA?   11.____

     A. Molybdenum
     B. Aluminum
     C. Sodium
     D. Zinc

12. At low turbidity levels, the most efficient viral removal treatment is   12.____

     A. coagulation/flocculation
     B. filtration
     C. settling
     D. disinfection

13. Which of the following compounds would contribute to the "temporary hardness" of water?   13.____

    A. Magnesium carbonate
    B. Sodium bicarbonate
    C. Potassium carbonate
    D. Calcium chloride

14. Which of the following coagulants may be objectionable in a distribution system, due to problems with steam boilers?   14.____

    A. Calcite or whiting
    B. Liquid alum
    C. Quicklime
    D. Activated silica

15. Which of the following is named by the EPA as the best available technology for removing fluoride?   15.____

    A. Electrodialysis
    B. Anion exchange resins
    C. Modified lime softening
    D. Activated alumina adsorption

16. For rapid sand filtration, the minimum filtration rate should be set at about _____ gal/sq.ft/min.   16.____

    A. 2
    B. 20
    C. 35
    D. 80

17. The liquid chromatographic post-column fluorescence method, according to Standard Methods, is an acceptable analysis for detecting the presence of   17.____

    A. extractable base/neutrals and acids
    B. volatile halocarbons
    C. polynuclear aromatic hydrocarbons
    D. glyphosate herbicides

18. The data on a plant's inventory cards typically include   18.____
       I. equipment inventory numbers
     II. equipment schedule numbers
    III. maintenance schedules
    IV. any maintenance work orders or reports

    A. I and II
    B. I and III
    C. II, III and IV
    D. I, II, III and IV

19. Which of the following is a volatile organic compound? 19._____

    A. Vinyl chloride
    B. Carbolic acid
    C. Toluene
    D. Atrazine

20. The most effective methods for removing arsenic from drinking water include each of the 20._____
following, EXCEPT

    A. activated aluminum
    B. coagulation with filtration
    C. ion exchange
    D. electrodialysis

21. Typically, the minimum detention time required for the settling process is _____ hour(s). 21._____

    A. 1
    B. 2
    C. 4
    D. 6

22. Which of the following is a base monitoring requirement for trihalomethanes (THMs)? 22._____

    A. In the system, a minimum of 50% of samples taken at the maximum residence time
    B. In the system, 50% of samples taken at named representative locations
    C. A minimum of 4 samples per quarter at treatment plants
    D. A minimum of 1 sample per quarter at treatment plants

23. What is the EPA's maximum contaminant level (MCL, in mg/L) for selenium? 23._____

    A. 0.005
    B. 0.050
    C. 0.500
    D. 5.000

24. "Breakpoint" is a term that applies to the process of 24._____

    A. Coagulation/flocculation
    B. Fluoridation
    C. Ion exchange
    D. Chlorination

25. For soft waters, the pH range generally required for best coagulation results is about 25._____

    A. 5.2-6.0
    B. 5.8-6.4
    C. 6.8-7.8
    D. 7.2-8.0

KEY (CORRECT ANSWERS)

1.	A		11.	A
2.	C		12.	D
3.	C		13.	A
4.	C		14.	D
5.	B		15.	D
6.	B		16.	A
7.	A		17.	D
8.	C		18.	A
9.	A		19.	A
10.	D		20.	B

21.	C
22.	C
23.	B
24.	D
25.	B

TEST 2

DIRECTIONS: Each question or incomplete statement is followed by several suggested answers or completions. Select the one the BEST answers the question or completes the statement. *PRINT THE LETTER OF THE CORRECT ANSWER IN THE SPACE AT THE RIGHT.*

1. Which of the following traditional treatment processes is most effective at removing volatile compounds?   1._____

   A. Chlorination
   B. Activated carbon treatment
   C. Coagulation
   D. Aeration

2. Which of the following is classified as a chemical treatment?   2._____

   A. Coagulation
   B. Water softening
   C. Diatomaceous filtration
   D. Activated carbon treatment

3. Factors which influence the surface load of a sedimentation basin include   3._____
   I.   depth
   II. width
   III. flow
   IV. length

   A. I, II and IV
   B. I and III
   C. II and IV
   D. I, II, III and IV

4. Major goals of removing settleable particles from raw waters include the reduction of each of the following, EXCEPT   4._____

   A. hardness
   B. turbidity
   C. color
   D. pH

5. Of the following, which complaint is most often reported by consumers of drinking water?   5._____

   A. Fishy odor
   B. Cloudy appearance
   C. Chlorine taste
   D. Off-color appearance

6. Pretreatment storage in an artificial tank is particularly effective when raw water is derived from a(n)   6._____

   A. lake   B. river   C. aquifer   D. well

7. Under the Safe Drinking Water Act, the minimum and maximum allowable pH range for potability is   7.____

  A. 4-9
  B. 5.5-8.6
  C. 6.5 - 8.5
  D. 7.0 - 7.8

8. Of the following treatments, which would normally be selected for organic contaminants?   8.____

  A. Ion exchange
  B. Activated alumina
  C. Reverse osmosis
  D. Packed-tower aeration

9. Which of the following inorganic chemicals is LEAST likely to appear in a drinking water supply?   9.____

  A. Sulfate
  B. Zinc
  C. Aluminum
  D. Nickel

10. Oxygen's content in water is approximately _____% of the dissolved gases.   10.____

  A. 17
  B. 38
  C. 54
  D. 72

11. Advantages of hard water over soft water generally include   11.____
      I.   Less likely to produce scale in hot water pipes and heaters
      II. Less danger of corrosivity
      III. Better taste

  A. I only
  B. I and II
  C. II and III
  D. I, II and III

12. Flocs are removed from water by the process of   12.____

  A. filtration
  B. coagulation
  C. disinfection
  D. sedimentation

13. When no other raw water source is available and hardness is at or above _____ ppm, softening should be considered.   13._____

    A. 50
    B. 100
    C. 150
    D. 200

14. Each of the following assumptions can be considered reasonable in the calculation of the   14._____
Accepted Daily Intake (ADI) or Adjusted Acceptable Daily Intake (AADI) of a chemical or compound, EXCEPT

    A. The target of the acceptable daily intake is the Suggested No-Adverse-Response-Level (SNARL)
    B. When insufficient data are available for air and food contamination, a 20% contribution from drinking water is typically used in preparing standards
    C. Water intake used in formulas is of 2 liters (2.11 quarts) per day
    D. An adult of 70 kg (154 lb.) is computed in health-related formulas

15. Packed-tower stripping is the only EPA-named "best available technology" for the   15._____
removal of

    A. benzene
    B. vinyl chloride
    C. asbestos
    D. dioxin

16. In general, the treatment period required for flocculation is about   16._____

    A. 5-10 minutes
    B. 10-30 minutes
    C. 30-60 minutes
    D. 1-2 hours

17. In nature, mercury occurs rarely in a free state, but usually in combination with   17._____

    A. silver
    B. sulfur
    C. iron
    D. oxygen

18. According to Standard Methods, which of the following tests is appropriate method of   18._____
analysis for carbamate pesticides?

    A. High performance liquid chromatography
    B. Purge-and-trap capillary column gas chromatography
    C. Purge-and-trap mass spectrometry
    D. Volumetric method

19. Which of the following is LEAST likely to occur as a waterborne disease?   19._____

    A. Typhoid   B. Cholera
    C. Infectious hepatitis   D. Diarrhea/enteritis

20. In order to assure proper functioning of the retention tank and auxiliary pumping compo- 20.____
nents, it is important for a dissolved air flotation (DAF) system to be operated between
the design pressure specifications of _____ psi.

    A. 10-20
    B. 25-50
    C. 40-90
    D. 75-120

21. In the International System of Units (SI), which of the following is the unit of absolute vis- 21.____
cosity?

    A. Stoke
    B. Brix
    C. Poise
    D. Gill

22. For raw waters high in color, the pH range generally required for best coagulation results 22.____
is about

    A. 5.0-6.0
    B. 5.8-6.4
    C. 6.8-7.8
    D. 7.0-8.0

23. Which of the following is a Class A carcinogen, as classified by the EPA? 23.____

    A. Arsenic
    B. Cadmium
    C. PCBs
    D. Toluene

24. Which of the following types of water analyses requires the shortest maximum holding 24.____
time?

    A. Phenolics
    B. Organic carbon
    C. Turbidity
    D. pH

25. Water depth over the filtration media should be maintained at about _____feet. 25.____

    A. 4-5
    B. 7-10
    C. 12-16
    D. 18-25

KEY (CORRECT ANSWERS)

1.	D		11.	C
2.	B		12.	A
3.	D		13.	C
4.	D		14.	A
5.	C		15.	B
6.	B		16.	B
7.	C		17.	B
8.	D		18.	A
9.	C		19.	C
10.	B		20.	C

21.	C
22.	A
23.	A
24.	D
25.	A

TEST 3

DIRECTIONS: Each question or incomplete statement is followed by several suggested answers or completions. Select the one the BEST answers the question or completes the statement. *PRINT THE LETTER OF THE CORRECT ANSWER IN THE SPACE AT THE RIGHT.*

1. Which of the following is NOT typically included in the operational record of a water treatment plant?   1._____

    A.   Units not in service
    B.   Time of coagulant application
    C.   Quantity of chemicals used in treatment
    D.   Time of sampling

2. The desirable upper limit of total solids in a public water supply is _____mg/L.   2._____

    A.   150
    B.   500
    C.   750
    D.   1000

3. Which of the following is a disadvantage associated with chlorination at several points from intake to distribution?   3._____

    A.   Ineffective bactericidal treatment
    B.   Inability to adapt to a sudden deterioration of quality
    C.   High dosage requirements
    D.   Complexity of construction

4. Under the EPA's Phase II rules, sampling for synthetic organic compounds must occur   4._____

    A.   once, during the first year only
    B.   once each year for surface water and once every three years for groundwater
    C.   quarterly for the first year, annually after that, and then every 3 years if not detected
    D.   once for four consecutive quarters

5. In industrialized nations such as the United States, the average daily water consumption is generally between _____ gallons per capita per day.   5._____

    A.   14 to 65
    B.   67 to 140
    C.   92 to 225
    D.   136 to 360

6. Which of the following is NOT a by-product of ozonation?   6._____

    A.   Epoxides
    B.   Trihalomethanes (THMs)
    C.   Unsaturated aldehydes
    D.   Organic peroxides

7. Which of the following compounds has the lowest maximum contaminant level(MCL, in mg/L) assigned by the EPA?

    A. Chlordane
    B. Styrene
    C. Carbon tetrachloride .005
    D. Toluene

7.____

8. Which of the following is NOT approved as a heterotrophic plate count method?

    A. Spread plate
    B. Membrane filter
    C. multiple-tube fermentation
    D. Pour plate

8.____

9. Under the Safe Drinking Water Act, the standard for acceptable color in drinking water is _____ total color units (TCU).

    A. 5
    B. 15
    C. 30
    D. 50

9.____

10. Conventional ion exchange units operate about the same as

    A. sludge scrapers
    B. solids-contact units
    C. flocculation basins
    D. downflow granular filters

10.____

11. The expected surface loading rate (SLR) during activated carbon treatment is usually _____ gpm/sq.ft.

    A. 2-5
    B. 5-12
    C. 10-15
    D. 12-22

11.____

12. Which of the following is NOT considered to be a reliable method for determining fluorine ion concentration?

    A. Dithizone method
    B. Complexone method
    C. Ion selective electrode method
    D. Colorimetric method

12.____

13. Which of the following is generally insoluble once oxidized in a solution with a pH of 7-8.5?

    A. Sodium
    B. Iron
    C. Chlorine
    D. Manganese

13.____

14. Which of the following chlorine compounds is NOT typically applied for the purpose of disinfection?   14.____

    A. Chlorine dioxide
    B. Chlorine gas
    C. Chlorite
    D. Hypochlorite

15. Which of the following inorganic chemicals is NOT carginogenic?   15.____

    A. Chromium
    B. Selenium
    C. Fluoride
    D. Cadmium

16. Monitoring for man-made radionuclides is required for surface water systems serving _____ persons or more.   16.____

    A. 10,000
    B. 40,000
    C. 100,000
    D. 400,000

17. Large-sized filter beds in treatment plants are generally limited to between _____mc/ day.   17.____

    A. 1,000-5,000
    B. 1,000-14,000
    C. 2,000-40,000
    D. 3,000-60,000

18. What is considered to be the reasonable range (mg/L) of sodium content in a water supply?   18.____

    A. 0.05-0.20
    B. 0.1-0.2
    C. 5-15
    D. 20-200

19. Which of the following coagulants is most effective when the water to be treated is not sufficiently alkaline?   19.____

    A. Activated silica
    B. Soda ash
    C. Liquid alum
    D. Ferric chloride

20. According to the federal Criteria for Evaluation and Standards Specifications, which of the following is classified as a Type C inorganic chemical?   20.____

    A. Lead
    B. Potassium
    C. Cyanide
    D. Zinc

21. The volumetric method, according to Standard Methods, is an acceptable analysis for detecting the presence of

    A. acidic herbicides
    B. methane
    C. PCBs
    D. phenols

    21._____

22. Any tap in a system used as a sampling point should be without attachment, and should run for a minimum of _____ or more.

    A. 10 seconds
    B. 30 seconds
    C. 2 minutes
    D. 10 minutes

    22._____

23. Aromatic compounds generally include

    A. esters
    B. halides
    C. ketones
    D. ethers

    23._____

24. During coagulation, operational limits generally require that alum dosage be maintained between _____ ppm.

    A. 5-10
    B. 10-50
    C. 50-100
    D. 100-200

    24._____

25. "Plain sedimentation" occurs when

    A. coagulation is eliminated
    B. disinfection is eliminated
    C. filtration is eliminated
    D. there is no in take-to-output flow

    25._____

———————

KEY (CORRECT ANSWERS)

1.	D	11.	A
2.	B	12.	A
3.	B	13.	B
4.	C	14.	C
5.	C	15.	C
6.	B	16.	C
7.	C	17.	C
8.	B	18.	D
9.	B	19.	B
10.	D	20.	B

21.	B
22.	C
23.	C
24.	B
25.	A

EXAMINATION SECTION
TEST 1

DIRECTIONS: Each question or incomplete statement is followed by several suggested answers or completions. Select the one the BEST answers the question or completes the statement. *PRINT THE LETTER OF THE CORRECT ANSWER IN THE SPACE AT THE RIGHT.*

1. In general, the most economic means of removing excess copper from water is   1.____

    A. reverse osmosis
    B. ion exchange
    C. lime softening
    D. coagulation/filtration

2. The EPA's rules on sampling for coliforms require a minimum standard sampling volume   2.____
of _____ ml.

    A. 50
    B. 100
    C. 200
    D. 500

3. Which of the following processes typically occurs LATEST in the water treatment   3.____
sequence?

    A. Activated carbon treatment
    B. Eutrophication control
    C. Flocculation
    D. Iron/Manganese control

4. In terms of water quality, "true color" refers to the color of a sample   4.____

    A. under ultraviolet light
    B. of raw water
    C. that has undergone direct filtration
    D. with turbidity removed

5. What is considered to be a reasonable range of concentration (mg/L) for iodine in drink-   5.____
ing water?

    A. 0.5-1.0
    B. 10-12
    C. 75-150
    D. 250-600

6. Which of the following disinfecting agents involves the danger of explosive tendency?   6.____

    A. Chloramine
    B. Ozone
    C. Sodium hypochlorite
    D. Chlorine dioxide

7. When the alkalinity of a water sample is less than the hardness, the existing salts of calcium and magnesium are likely to be

    A. sulfates instead of carbonates
    B. bicarbonates
    C. carbonates instead of sulfates
    D. negligible

7.____

8. Which of the following coagulants is often used in the treatment of very cold water?

    A. Hydrated lime
    B. Filter alum
    C. Activated silica
    D. Sodium aluminate

8.____

9. After the initial agitation, controlled agitation for coagulation should be maintained at a rate of about _____ ft/sec.

    A. 0.1-0.3
    B. 0.2-0.6
    C. 0.5-2.0
    D. 3.0-5.0

9.____

10. According to the federal Criteria for Evaluation and Standards Specifications, which of the following is classified as a Type A inorganic chemical?

    A. Sodium
    B. Tin
    C. Copper
    D. Iron

10.____

11. Which of the following should NEVER be added before lime soda softening or ion exchange?

    A. Polyelectrolytes
    B. Fluoride compound
    C. Activated alumina
    D. Chlorine compound

11.____

12. The usual process for the removal of iron and manganese from water is

    A. Aeration
    B. Downflow granular filtration
    C. Sedimentation
    D. Coagulation/flocculation

12.____

13. Turbidity is a characteristic mostly caused by the presence of _____ matter in water.

    A. ionized
    B. crystalloid
    C. molecular
    D. colloidal

13.____

14. Ideally, filter backwashing should be scheduled on the basis of   14.____
    A. volume treated
    B. time
    C. head loss
    D. post-filtration contamination

15. According to federal regulations, any water beneath the surface of the ground with signif-   15.____
    icant and rapid shifts in characteristics such as turbidity, temperature, pH, or conductivity
    with closely correlates to climatological conditions is defined as
    A. contaminated water
    B. groundwater above the water table
    C. groundwater under the direct influence of surface water
    D. raw water

16. For taste and odor control, powdered activated carbon is normally introduced   16.____
    A. before aeration
    B. after softening
    C. before coagulation
    D. after filtration

17. In the context of water treatment, the most important sodium compound found in water is   17.____
    A. borax
    B. sodium phosphate
    C. sodium bicarbonate
    D. common salt (sodium chloride)

18. If volatile organic compounds are not detected in groundwater, the EPA still requires   18.____
    source testing every
    A. quarter
    B. year
    C. 3 years
    D. 5 years

19. Organic substances such as humic and fulvic acids are coagulated by   19.____
    A. soda ash
    B. calcite and polyelectrolytes
    C. iron and aluminum salts
    D. bentonite or Fuller's earth

20. Which of the following compounds has the lowest maximum contaminant level (MCL, in   20.____
    mg/L) assigned by the EPA?
    A. Glyphosate
    B. Xylene
    C. Benzene
    D. Dioxin

21. To prevent the formation of currents and breaking of floc during settling, the overflow rate should not exceed _____ gal/day/ft of weir length.

    A. 170
    B. 540
    C. 12,300
    D. 20,000

21.____

22. Which of the following chemicals has some nutritional value in small quantities?

    A. Arsenic
    B. Cadmium
    C. Nitrate
    D. Lead

22.____

23. In a raw water with a concentration of 100-300 mg/L of suspended solids, a 50% removal is typically accomplished with a detention time during sedimentation of _____ hour(s).

    A. 0.5-1.0
    B. 1.0-1.5
    C. 2.0-4.0
    D. 4.0-6.0

23.____

24. According to Standard Methods, which of the following tests is an appropriate method of analysis for disinfection by-products?

    A. Volumetric method
    B. Combustible-gas indicator method
    C. Micro liquid-liquid extraction gas chromatography
    D. Purge-and-trap gas column gas chromatography

24.____

25. The use of fine screens in drawing raw water from pretreatment storage serves to inter-cept large and fine solids, and involves the additional advantage of

    A. moderate aeration
    B. lowering organic content
    C. enhancing the life of filters
    D. improving the efficiency of coagulation

25.____

KEY (CORRECT ANSWERS)

1.	C		11.	B
2.	B		12.	A
3.	D		13.	D
4.	D		14.	C
5.	A		15.	C
6.	B		16.	C
7.	A		17.	D
8.	D		18.	D
9.	C		19.	C
10.	C		20.	D

21.	D
22.	A
23.	B
24.	C
25.	D

———

TEST 2

DIRECTIONS: Each question or incomplete statement is followed by several suggested answers or completions. Select the one the BEST answers the question or completes the statement. *PRINT THE LETTER OF THE CORRECT ANSWER IN THE SPACE AT THE RIGHT.*

1.   The operation of a public water supply system is   1.____

    A.   recorded and reported daily
    B.   recorded daily and reported monthly
    C.   recorded weekly and reported monthly
    D.   recorded and reported monthly

2.   The most commonly used dechlorinating agent, both in treatment and sampling, is   2.____

    A.   sodium thiosulfate
    B.   acetone
    C.   calcium carbonate
    D.   chlorine dioxide

3.   Which of the following substances, at a low concentration, will impart a swampy, musty   3.____
odor to drinking water?

    A.   Hydrogen sulfide
    B.   E. coli
    C.   Calcium carbonate
    D.   Lead

4.   Which of the following traditional treatment processes contributes the most to corrosion   4.____
in the distribution system?

    A.   Water softening
    B.   Coagulation/Flocculation
    C.   Sedimentation
    D.   Aeration

5.   Which of the following terms is an expression of the concentration of calcium and mag-   5.____
nesium ions in water?

    A.   Turbidity
    B.   Alkalinity
    C.   Settleable solids
    D.   Hardness

6.   The most effective coagulants for the removal of viruses from raw water are typically   6.____

    A.   copperas and chlorinated copperas
    B.   silica and clays
    C.   lime and calcite
    D.   alum and ferric chlorides

7. The Platinum-Cobalt Method is a means of   7.____

    A. ionization
    B. standardizing color
    C. reducing hardness
    D. fixing pH value

8. Generally, flow through settling basins should be maintained at or under _____ ft/sec.   8.____

    A. 0.5
    B. 1
    C. 3
    D. 5

9. Which of the following is NOT a process for removing turbidity from drinking water?   9.____

    A. Aeration
    B. Filtration
    C. Sedimentation
    D. Coagulation

10. Sampling program subdivisions routinely include each of the following, EXCEPT   10.____

    A. sampling points indicative of pretreatment, intermediate, and post-treatment
    B. distribution sampling
    C. raw water sampling
    D. biomatter sampling

11. The major consumer of chlorine in the first stage of disinfection is   11.____

    A. ammonia
    B. ozone
    C. free hydrogen
    D. sodium hydroxide

12. Which of the following is NOT a recommended treatment process for the removal of mercury?   12.____

    A. Reverse osmosis
    B. Activated alumina adsorption
    C. Granular activated carbon
    D. Lime softening

13. The processes available for desalination include each of the following, EXCEPT   13.____

    A. reverse osmosis
    B. ion exchange
    C. lime softening
    D. electrodialysis

14. What is the EPA's published maximum contaminant level goal (MCLG, in mg/L), for sulfate?   14.____

    A. 0.500   B. 5.000
    C. 50.00   D. 500.0

15. The EPA's rules on sampling for coliforms state under normal circumstances (when more than 40 samples per month are taken) state that not more than _____ sample(s) per month may be positive.

    A. 1
    B. 2
    C. 5
    D. 10

15.____

16. Which of the following statements about the lime-soda softening process is TRUE?

    A. A reduced feeding velocity is usually necessary.
    B. Disinfection by chlorination of softened water must be increased.
    C. Only brief flocculation is necessary.
    D. Sedimentation times between 1-2 hours are sufficient.

16.____

17. Which of the following treatment processes will have an effect on the barium level of a water supply?

    A. Rapid sand filtration
    B. Aeration
    C. Lime softening
    D. Coagulation

17.____

18. Which of the following coagulants is generally considered ineffective for colored waters?

    A. Copperas
    B. Calcite or whiting
    C. Ferric sulfate
    D. Clay

18.____

19. The most practical time to increase the chlorination of a water supply is

    A. after filtration and before chemical treatment
    B. at the effluent or final chlorination
    C. after chemical treatment but before fluoridation
    D. after settling and before filtration

19.____

20. The porosity of gravels used in rapid sand filters should remain between _____ %.

    A. 10-20
    B. 35-45
    C. 40-60
    D. 75-85

20.____

21. Which of the following chemicals' content in water is regulated by the EPA?

    A. Potassium
    B. Phosphorus
    C. Bromine
    D. Magnesium

21.____

22. Under EPA's "Phase I" requirements, initial sampling of a surface or groundwater source is required   22.____

    A. monthly
    B. quarterly
    C. biannually
    D. annually

23. Typically, filter washwater will account for about _____ % of the totalplant flow.   23.____

    A. 2-4
    B. 8-10
    C. 15-22
    D. 20-30

24. Which of the following is NOT a process in the disinfection of raw water that can eliminate trihalomethanes (THMs) such as chloroform?   24.____

    A. Coagulation
    B. Activated carbon
    C. Aeration
    D. Ozonation

25. The control of coagulation in the treatment process is significantly affected by each of the following, EXCEPT   25.____

    A. dissolved oxygen
    B. turbidity
    C. free carbon dioxide
    D. pH

_____

KEY (CORRECT ANSWERS)

1. B			11. A	
2. A			12. B	
3. A			13. C	
4. D			14. D	
5. D			15. C	
6. D			16. B	
7. B			17. C	
8. A			18. A	
9. A			19. D	
10. D			20. B	

21. C
22. B
23. A
24. A
25. A

TEST 3

DIRECTIONS: Each question or incomplete statement is followed by several suggested answers or completions. Select the one the BEST answers the question or completes the statement. *PRINT THE LETTER OF THE CORRECT ANSWER IN THE SPACE AT THE RIGHT.*

1. Which of the following processes is LEAST likely to be included in a solids-contact unit?   1._____

    A. Sedimentation
    B. Flocculation
    C. Rapid mixing
    D. Filtration

2. Water with applicable concentrations of 150-300 mg/L would be described as   2._____

    A. soft
    B. moderately hard
    C. hard
    D. very hard

3. Which of the following is a method of adsorption?   3._____

    A. Osmosis
    B. Iron/manganese removal
    C. Filtration
    D. Activated carbon treatment

4. Typically, the temperature of water sampled for a Taste Threshold Test should be at about _____ ° C.   4._____

    A. 15
    B. 30
    C. 45
    D. 60

5. Under the EPA's Phase II rules, sampling for asbestos must occur   5._____

    A. once, during the first year only
    B. once each year for surface water and once every three years for groundwater
    C. quarterly for the first year, annually after that, and then every 3 years if not detected
    D. quarterly for the first year, reduced to one per year after one round of no detection

6. Following mixing, operational limits generally require a detention time for coagulation and flocculation of between   6._____

    A. 10-15 minutes
    B. 15-45 minutes
    C. 1-2 hours
    D. 3-4 hours

7. pH values higher than 7 are generally expected in samples of raw water due to the presence of   7.____

   A. carbonates and bicarbonates
   B. oxides
   C. nitrates
   D. microbes

8. Which of the following chemicals has been assigned a maximum contaminant level goal (MCLG) by the EPA?   8.____

   A. Dissolved oxygen
   B. Calcium
   C. Ozone
   D. Iron

9. In general, multiple chlorination is effective when the quality of raw water is good--but the factor of safety is   9.____

   A. fluoridation
   B. coagulation/flocculation
   C. filtration
   D. pH control

10. Which of the following coagulants is effective in absorbing taste and odor substances?   10.____

   A. Hydrated lime
   B. Copperas
   C. Bentonite
   D. Filter alum

11. Which of the following is generally considered to me the most effective method for the removal of nitrates from water?   11.____

   A. Biological denitrification
   B. Lime softening
   C. Chemical coagulation
   D. Anion exchange

12. For coagulation, the generally-accepted minimum alkalinity of water under treatment is about _____ mg/L as $CaCO_3$.   12.____

   A. 5
   B. 10
   C. 20
   D. 40

13. In-plant analyses reveal a sulfate level that is unacceptably high. As a first and most economical alternative, the plant should consider   13.____

   A. dilution from other water supply sources
   B. reverse osmosis
   C. ion exchange
   D. the use of aluminum sulfate in the coagulation/flocculation process

14. Which of the following existing plant operations can help to achieve a goal of trihalom-   14.____
    ethane (THM) reduction at a relatively low cost?
        I.   Improved coagulation and settling through flocculant aids
        II. Chlorine dioxide treatment
        III. More frequent jar testing
        IV. Ozonation

    A. I and III
    B. I, II and IV
    C. III and IV
    D. I, II, III and IV

15. Which of the following is NOT typically used for pH adjustments to potable water?   15.____

    A. Soda ash
    B. Sodium silicate
    C. Caustic soda
    D. Lime

16. Which of the following physical parameters is a primary drinking water standard, as used   16.____
    by the EPA?

    A. Turbidity
    B. Corrosivity
    C. pH
    D. Total dissolved solids

17. The settling process is desirable for waters with a turbidity of _____ ppm or more.   17.____

    A. 10
    B. 30
    C. 50
    D. 100

18. Which of the following types of water analyses requires the use of a glass sampling bot-   18.____
    tle?

    A. Settleable matter
    B. Oil and grease
    C. Cyanides
    D. Conductance

19. The preferred method for the detection of cadmium in a water supply is the _____   19.____
    method.

    A. Neocuproine
    B. Atomic Absorption Spectrometric
    C. Colorimetric
    D. Dithizone

20. The *primary* advantage associated with the use of sodium hypochlorite for disinfection is that it   20.____

    A.   is odorless
    B.   requires less storage space than most other compounds
    C.   is safer to handle than most other compounds
    D.   is stored dry

21. For which of the following is evidence of carcinogenicity the strongest?   21.____

    A.   Styrene
    B.   PCBs
    C.   Toluene
    D.   Arsenic

22. The expected residual of free chlorine at the end of a distribution is about _____ mg/L.   22.____

    A.   .002
    B.   2
    C.   20
    D.   200

23. Because of its oxidation process and the consequent power to be virucidal, _____ is often a preferred disinfectant in the prechlorination process.   23.____

    A.   Ozone
    B.   Carbon dioxide
    C.   Sodium thiosulfate
    D.   Bromine

24. The fastest standardized method for the detection of coliforms is the   24.____

    A.   presence-absence (P-A) coliform test
    B.   membrane filter technique (MF)
    C.   minimal media (MMO-MUG) test
    D.   multiple-tube fermentation technique (MPN)

25. Which of the following is a precipitation treatment?   25.____

    A.   Deferrization
    B.   Fluoridation
    C.   Flocculation
    D.   Activated carbon treatment

KEY (CORRECT ANSWERS)

1.	D	11.	D
2.	C	12.	C
3.	D	13.	A
4.	A	14.	A
5.	A	15.	B
6.	B	16.	A
7.	A	17.	C
8.	D	18.	B
9.	C	19.	B
10.	C	20.	C

21.	B
22.	B
23.	A
24.	B
25.	A

———

EXAMINATION SECTION
TEST 1

DIRECTIONS: Each question or incomplete statement is followed by several suggested answers or completions. Select the one that BEST answers the question or completes the statement. *PRINT THE LETTER OF THE CORRECT ANSWER IN THE SPACE AT THE RIGHT.*

1. Water that is associated with the formation of rocks is classified as

    A. metamorphic   B. magmatic
    C. volcanic   D. plutonic

1.____

2. Which of the following sources of groundwater contamination would be classified as a *Category 5* source?

    A. Construction excavation
    B. Irrigation practices
    C. De-icing salts application
    D. Hazardous waste, land application

2.____

3. *Artesian* water is water that comes from

    A. underground springs
    B. a confined source
    C. just below the water table
    D. glacial outwash

3.____

4. Which of the following types of sedimentary rock has the HIGHEST porosity?

    A. Sandstone   B. Limestone   C. Shale   D. Siltstone

4.____

5. Contaminant withdrawal designed *specifically* for the removal of volatile compounds from the unsaturated zone is effected by use of

    A. pumping   B. interceptor systems
    C. soil venting   D. excavation

5.____

6. In a porous medium, heat is transported by each of the following processes EXCEPT

    A. conduction   B. advection
    C. radiation   D. convection

6.____

7. Pressure recovery in a borehole after the withdrawal of a known volume of water is termed _____ testing.

    A. time-drawdown   B. drillstem
    C. slug injection   D. borehole-dilution

7.____

8. Which of the following is NOT a fundamental purpose for the artificial recharge of a water source?

    A. Prevention or retardation of saltwater intrusion
    B. Replenishment of depleted supplies
    C. Maintenance of normal seismic conditions
    D. Underground storage to supplement inadequate surface-storage facilities

8.____

9. The method of hydraulic testing used to determine the seepage velocity of a groundwater resource is called   9.____

   A. borehole-dilution   B. distance-drawdown
   C. drill stem   D. slug injection

10. Mass transport caused by flow of water in which the mass is dissolved is termed   10.____

   A. dispersion   B. dissolution
   C. vectorization   D. advection

11. Water below the zone of saturation is classified as _____ water.   11.____

   A. subsurface   B. internal
   C. gravitational   D. interstitial

12. Each of the following is a factor in determining safe yield of a groundwater resource EXCEPT   12.____

   A. permissible cost of pumping
   B. average annual recharge
   C. advection rate
   D. water table level

13. Which of the following methods of hydraulic testing requires both a pumping well and an observation well?   13.____

   A. Drillstem   B. Slug injection
   C. Borehole-dilution   D. Time-drawdown

14. Which of the following contaminants is classified as a volatile?   14.____

   A. Arsenic   B. Phenol   C. Toluene   D. Chlordane

15. The DOMINANT nutrient contaminant in groundwater supplies is   15.____

   A. iron   B. nitrate   C. ammonium   D. phosphorus

16. Which of the following substances is NOT used in the age-dating of groundwater?   16.____

   A. Carbon-14   B. Tritium   C. Chlorine-36   D. Strontium

17. Natural material that stores water and transmits enough water to be significant in regional migration studies, but not enough to supply individual wells, is called   17.____

   A. aquiclude   B. aquifer   C. aquitard   D. aquifuge

18. The use of seeded bacteria to transform organic compounds into less hazardous compounds is an example of   18.____

   A. bioremediation   B. slug injection
   C. an interceptor system   D. artificial recharge

19. Contaminants described as light non-aqueous phase liquids (LNAPLs) are MOST often found   19.____

   A. at the top of the capillary fringe   B. in the saturated zone
   C. at the water table   D. in soil water

20. Each of the following is a major source of trace metal contamination in groundwater EXCEPT   20._____

    A. agricultural wastes   B. urban runoff
    C. subsurface percolation   D. fossil fuels

21. Another term for *permeability* is   21._____

    A. transmissivity   B. hydraulic conductivity
    C. flux   D. porosity

22. Which of the following materials would be found at the HIGHEST point in an alluvial fan deposit?   22._____

    A. Sand   B. Mud   C. Clay   D. Gravel

23. Water that is in or derived from a magma at a depth of several kilometers is classified as   23._____

    A. metamorphic   B. magmatic
    C. volcanic   D. plutonic

24. Which of the following factors would DIRECTLY influence the shape of a contaminant solute plume?   24._____

    A. Presence of sources or sinks
    B. Configuration of water table
    C. Hydraulic conductivity distribution within the flow field
    D. Shape of flow domain

25. Water returns through the atmosphere through each of the following processes EXCEPT   25._____

    A. volatilization   B. transpiration
    C. evaporation   D. sublimation

35

KEY (CORRECT ANSWERS)

1.	A	11.	B
2.	A	12.	C
3.	B	13.	D
4.	D	14.	C
5.	C	15.	B
6.	B	16.	D
7.	C	17.	C
8.	C	18.	A
9.	A	19.	A
10.	D	20.	C

21.	B
22.	D
23.	D
24.	C
25.	A

TEST 2

DIRECTIONS: Each question or incomplete statement is followed by several suggested answers or completions. Select the one that BEST answers the question or completes the statement. *PRINT THE LETTER OF THE CORRECT ANSWER IN THE SPACE AT THE RIGHT.*

1. _____ flow is NOT a component part of a hydrograph.   1._____

   A. Overland   B. Sub   C. Inter   D. Base

2. Which of the following is NOT an essential feature in determining the response of a basin to pumping?   2._____

   A. Distance to recharge area
   B. Configuration of cone of depression
   C. Character of recharge
   D. Distance to area of natural discharge

3. In a spreading basin, the hydraulic response to a recharge well MOST often takes the form of a   3._____

   A. mound   B. cone of impression
   C. cone of recharge   D. cone of depression

4. Which of the following is NOT an example of *point-source* contamination?   4._____

   A. Disposal pond
   B. Leaking storage tank
   C. Nitrate effluents form household disposal
   D. Sanitary landfill leachate

5. Which of the following sediments has the LOWEST porosity?   5._____

   A. Gravel   B. Clay   C. Silt   D. Sand

6. The MOST economical method of water sampling for near-surface investigations in non-cohesive sand or silts is the _____ method.   6._____

   A. conventional standpipe nest
   B. movable packer arrangement
   C. multilevel, single borehole
   D. single level, single borehole

7. The rate of flow of water at a prevailing temperature through a vertical strip of aquifer extending the full saturated thickness of the aquifer is a measure known as   7._____

   A. head   B. transmissivity
   C. hydraulic potential   D. conductivity

8. Each of the following is an advantage associated with the use of piezometer nests for water sampling procedures, as opposed to single-borehole methods, EXCEPT   8._____

   A. relative durability   B. lower cost
   C. ease in measuring water level   D. less difficulty in seal installation

9. Which of the following materials has the HIGHEST permeability?   9.____

    A. Sandstone
    B. Silt
    C. Fractured crystalline rock
    D. Well-sorted gravel

10. Of the following sources of groundwater contamination, a(n) _____ be classified as a   10.____
    Category 4 source.

    A. open dump   B. saltwater intrusion
    C. mine drainage   D. septic tank

11. Which of the following materials would have the HIGHEST specific yield?   11.____

    A. Dune sand   B. Peat
    C. Sandstone   D. Limestone

12. The specific _____ of a water resource is expressed as a ratio of the volume of water   12.____
    that drains by gravity to the total volume of rock in the aquifer.

    A. yield   B. capacity   C. retention   D. storage

13. If an aquifer is bounded by a stream that provides recharge, the effect will be   13.____

    A. the production of another constant-head boundary
    B. a decrease in specific yield
    C. a decrease in well drawdown
    D. an increase in well drawdown

14. The saturated zone is separated from soil water by the _____ zone.   14.____

    A. intermediate   B. vadose
    C. phreatic   D. interstitial

15. Which of the following is an isotope that does NOT naturally appear in water?   15.____

    A. H_2 B. H_3 C. O_{14} D. O_{17}

16. Each of the following is a factor determining the vertical stress associated with basin   16.____
    loading EXCEPT

    A. hydraulic gradient
    B. depth
    C. density of saturated rock
    D. acceleration due to gravity

17. What is the term for subsurface rock which stores water but does not transmit significant   17.____
    amounts?

    A. Aquiclude   B. Aquifer   C. Aquitard   D. Aquifuge

18. Water that has never been in contact with the hydrosphere is classified as 18.____

    A. juvenile   B. metamorphic
    C. connate   D. plutonic

19. Mass is spread beyond the region it normally would occupy, due to lateral flow, through the process of 19.____

    A. volatilization   B. dispersion
    C. dissolution   D. advection

20. Which of the following is NOT an example of organic priority pollutants? 20.____

    A. Trace metals   B. Volatiles
    C. Acid extractables   D. Pesticides

21. In any region bound in part by a constant head, the flow must be directed 21.____

    A. at 45-degree angles from or toward the boundary
    B. upward or downward at angles not exceeding 60 degrees
    C. in lines parallel to the boundary lines
    D. at right angles from or toward the boundary

22. Which type of rock fractures are normal to each other, and not related to a single stress state? 22.____

    A. Conjugate   B. Schematic
    C. Regional   D. Orthogonal

23. The method of contaminant withdrawal used *specifically* to collect contaminant close to the water table is 23.____

    A. pumping   B. interceptor systems
    C. soil venting   D. excavation

24. Regions where the flow of water is directed *downward* with respect to the water table are classified as _____ areas. 24.____

    A. influent   B. recharge   C. effluent   D. discharge

25. Streams that lose water to a groundwater reservoir are classified as 25.____

    A. effluent   B. base   C. influent   D. runoff

KEY (CORRECT ANSWERS)

1. B	11. B
2. B	12. A
3. A	13. C
4. C	14. A
5. A	15. C
6. C	16. A
7. B	17. A
8. B	18. A
9. D	19. B
10. C	20. A

21. D
22. D
23. B
24. B
25. C

EXAMINATION SECTION
TEST 1

DIRECTIONS: Each question or incomplete statement is followed by several suggested answers or completions. Select the one that BEST answers the question or completes the statement. *PRINT THE LETTER OF THE CORRECT ANSWER IN THE SPACE AT THE RIGHT.*

1. Which of the following materials used in collecting water samples is LEAST likely to contribute contaminants to the sample?　　　　1.____

    A. Glass　　　　　　　　　　　　B. Teflon
    C. Polypropylene　　　　　　　　D. Stainless steel

2. A prepared reference sample, inserted into sample processing as close to the beginning as possible, is known as a(n) _____ sample.　　　　2.____

    A. audit　　　　　　　　　　　　B. control
    C. continuous　　　　　　　　　D. blank

3. Which type of sampling plan is based on the judgment of technical experts?　　　　3.____

    A. Intuitive　　　　　　　　　　B. Statistical
    C. Isokinetic　　　　　　　　　D. Spatial

4. Of the following, the type of *blank* NOT generally used in laboratory analysis is　　　　4.____

    A. solvent　　　　B. system　　　　C. method　　　　D. trip

5. An analyst should MOST strenuously avoid imposing turbulence on water samples that are being tested for　　　　5.____

    A. dissolved solids　　　　　　　B. biotic content
    C. dissolved gases　　　　　　　D. suspended particulates

6. Which of the following is NOT a primary factor in determining the appropriate device to be used in collecting air samples?　　　　6.____

    A. The amount of air to be moved
    B. Altitude of measurement
    C. Opposing vacuum forces
    D. Nature of substance to be analyzed

7. _____ meters is GENERALLY considered to be the shallowest depth in a standing body of water that will assure an analyst of the absence of chemical or thermal stratification.　　　　7.____

    A. 3　　　　　B. 5　　　　　C. 10　　　　　D. 15

8. The FIRST collection of any material for analysis is known as _____ sampling.　　　　8.____

    A. reference　　　　　　　　　　B. primary
    C. dip　　　　　　　　　　　　　D. control

9. The collection technique ESPECIALLY appropriate for sampling rivers for chemical constituents is　　　　9.____

    A. static grab　　　　　　　　　B. point sampling
    C. spatial gradient　　　　　　　D. stratified dip

10. To insure initial air flow through sampling and analyzing equipment, air pollutant samples   10.____
should be collected

    A.   on the upstream side of the air mover
    B.   as close to the air mover as possible
    C.   on the downstream side of the air mover
    D.   as far from the air mover as possible

11. The MINIMUM number of samples to be collected from a water distribution system is   11.____
determined by the

    A.   population served by the system
    B.   capacity of the system
    C.   linear range of distribution
    D.   peak rate of distribution

12. A substance that is being measured or sought in any sample of environmental or chemi-   12.____
cal matter is called a(n)

    A.   control   B.   reagent   C.   solvent   D.   analyte

13. The volume of air in a high-volume sample is measured in terms of   13.____

    A.   cubic meters
    B.   proportion of dissolved gases to ambient air
    C.   time lapsed during collection
    D.   rate of flow through the collection device

14. Which is the BEST season, in temperate regions, to collect samples from lakes in which   14.____
waters are mixed enough to allow representative readings?

    A.   Winter   B.   Spring   C.   Summer   D.   Fall

15. The standard, generalized method for separating a pollutant for analysis from an air sam-   15.____
ple is to

    A.   impose gravitational separators
    B.   use liquid media
    C.   exploit differences in related substances
    D.   leave the substances together, but catalog them with separate data

16. The ONLY accurate way to measure the content of waste-water samples is through the   16.____
analysis of

    A.   specific point samples
    B.   grab samples from areas that are well-mixed
    C.   samples from both upstream and downstream sides of the dump
    D.   composite samples that are proportioned according to flow patterns

17. A pool of two increments that is reduced or prepared as a subsample for analysis is   17.____
called a

    A.   spike   B.   gross sample
    C.   control sample   D.   continuous sample

18. Of the following, the one which is NOT an advantage associated with the use of static   18.____
    sensors in the collection of air samples is

    A. no requisite human supervision
    B. low cost
    C. high-volume efficiency rate
    D. operation without reliance on electrical power

19. A substance that absorbs and separates a contaminant from the remainder of a sample   19.____
    is a

    A. reactant   B. reagent   C. spike   D. control

20. When wastewater samples are being collected in order to appraise plant performance,   20.____
    the recommended sampling pattern consists of

    A. grab samples from different points during peak flow
    B. grab samples at regular time intervals over a random six-hour period
    C. composite samples over a 24-hour weekday period
    D. daily composite samples over a random seven-day period

21. One DISADVANTAGE associated with the use of dustfall jars for the collection of air sam-   21.____
    ples is

    A. dependence on supervision
    B. limited long-range collection
    C. expensive operation
    D. failure to measure smaller particles

22. The MOST effective method for removing potential contaminants from equipment used in   22.____
    sample collection is

    A. steam washing   B. repeated boiling
    C. inert disinfectants   D. detergent scrubbing

23. The term for a sample value that disagrees in magnitude with its neighboring samples is   23.____

    A. variance   B. spatial outlier
    C. spike   D. range

24. Which of the following is a method for measuring particulate pollution in air samples?   24.____

    A. Bubbling
    B. Adsorption
    C. Introduction of a reactant
    D. Inertial separation

25. Compounds whose presence obscures the measurement of a substance by introducing   25.____
    an unrelated analytical signal are referred to as

    A. interferences   B. controls
    C. toxics   D. blanks

KEY (CORRECT ANSWERS)

1.	B		11.	A
2.	A		12.	D
3.	A		13.	D
4.	D		14.	A
5.	C		15.	C
6.	B		16.	D
7.	B		17.	B
8.	B		18.	C
9.	C		19.	B
10.	A		20.	C

21.	D
22.	A
23.	B
24.	D
25.	A

TEST 2

DIRECTIONS: Each question or incomplete statement is followed by several suggested answers or completions. Select the one that BEST answers the question or completes the statement. *PRINT THE LETTER OF THE CORRECT ANSWER IN THE SPACE AT THE RIGHT.*

1. To determine the maximum load for a given wastewater treatment unit, an analyst should use _____ samples _____ flow.   1.____

    A.   grab; collected during peak
    B.   integrated; proportioned to the average
    C.   integrated; that reflect the range in
    D.   integrated; collected during peak

2. The AVERAGE rate of flow, in cubic feet per minute, through a mechanical air sampler is   2.____

    A.   10-20   B.   40-60   C.   100-130   D.   180-200

3. The obtaining of a representative sample from a flowing stream that contains particulate matter is known as _____ sampling.   3.____

    A.   stratified   B.   intuitive
    C.   isokinetic   D.   suspended

4. Of the following situations, the one MOST appropriate for the use of mechanical air samplers is for measuring   4.____

    A.   a high volume of particulate matter
    B.   dissolved gas content
    C.   a specific chemical substance
    D.   and separating particulate matter by size

5. The CORRECT term for introduced samples in a procedure that do not contain the substance of interest, but are otherwise composed the same as actual samples, is   5.____

    A.   controls   B.   spikes   C.   fields   D.   blanks

6. The number of sampling replications required to sufficient-ly characterize a water body is decided PRIMARILY by the   6.____

    A.   size of the water body
    B.   stratification of the water body
    C.   climatic conditions influencing the state of the water body
    D.   purpose of the sampling

7. When sampling is done for the purpose of monitoring quality, sample replication can be expressed in terms of each of the following EXCEPT   7.____

    A.   confidence limits   B.   arithmetic means
    C.   expanded controls   D.   standard deviations

8. The MOST common method for measuring the amount of particulate matter in an air sample is   8._____

    A. weighing the sampler's filter before and after collection
    B. recording level of chemical activity with an introduced reactant
    C. determining volume ratios based on the rate of flow
    D. a strictly calibrated volume measurement

9. The use of single point samples in wastewater analysis is considered ACCEPTABLE in the determination of   9._____

    A. the capacity of the system
    B. specific chemical substance content
    C. representative waste flow during operation hours
    D. compliance with discharge regulations

10. Which of the following types of water bodies contains the HIGHEST variability of chemical constituents?   10._____

    A. Freshwater lakes
    B. Near-shore marine environments
    C. Deep, rapidly flowing streams
    D. Shallow, slowly flowing streams

11. The type of sample against which the results of a procedure are judged is known as a(n)   11._____

    A. blank   B. spike   C. control   D. analyte

12. The MOST common method for removing dissolved gases from a given air sample is through   12._____

    A. adsorption with solids
    B. absorption into a liquid medium
    C. inertial separation
    D. filtration

13. In collecting samples from relatively shallow, rapidly flowing streams and rivers, an analyst should be aware that such streams   13._____

    A. contain widely varying constituents at different depths
    B. cannot be representatively sampled
    C. are not consistently stratified
    D. can be sufficiently sampled at one point

14. In sampling wastewater, the term for the time period or volume of waste for which a composite estimate is desired is the   14._____

    A. spatial gradient   B. composite range
    C. minimum range   D. primary sampling unit

15. The type of introduced sample used PRIMARILY by analysts as tools for assessing and controlling sample contamination is   15._____

    A. blanks   B. interferences
    C. reagents   D. controls

16. Which sampling pattern is the MOST commonly used in the monitoring of sewer use?   16.____

   A. Long-term composite samples at a point far downstream from the discharge
   B. Grab samples from different critical points in the system
   C. Composite samples from a point as close to the primary discharge as possible
   D. Composite samples from different critical points in the system

17. The one of the following sampling/collecting materials MOST likely to contribute a chloro-form contaminant to a water sample is   17.____

   A. fiberglas-reinforced epoxy (FRE)
   B. threaded PVC conduit
   C. polypropylene
   D. cemented PVC conduit

18. The MOST common motivation for sealing samples in their collection vessels is   18.____

   A. analysis of clear biotic potential
   B. prevention of dissolving particulate matter
   C. analysis of volatile compound content
   D. prevention of contamination from ambient air

19. If seasonal variations are of interest in a given water supply, monitoring samples should be collected   19.____

   A. hourly   B. daily   C. weekly   D. monthly

20. Which of the following types of *blanks* is NOT generally used in field collecting?   20.____

   A. Sampling media   B. Reagent
   C. Equipment   D. Matched-matrix

21. The collection medium for MOST high-volume air samplers is a   21.____

   A. borosilicate glass collection jar
   B. silica gel absorber
   C. glass fiber filter
   D. distilled, inert liquid

22. Of the following situations, the one which is MOST appropriate for the use of static sensors in the process of collection air samples is for   22.____

   A. collecting a specific volume of air
   B. separating sample content throughout time gradients
   C. measuring dissolved gases
   D. long-term collection of particulates

23. A deep, rapidly flowing river is _____ stratified _____ .   23.____

   A. usually; into fairly consistent thermal zones
   B. more likely to be; thermally than chemically
   C. more likely to be; than a standing body of water
   D. more likely to be; chemically than thermally

24. The type of sampling plan MOST likely to provide a basis for making probabilistic conclusions that are independent of personal judgment is   24.____

    A. statistical   B. isokinetic
    C. primary   D. intuitive

25. Generally, the BEST location from which to collect representative samples from smooth-flowing rivers that are above any tidal influences is at   25.____

    A. the surface   B. near-shore eddies
    C. mid-depth   D. lower depths

KEY (CORRECT ANSWERS)

1.	D		11.	C
2.	B		12.	B
3.	C		13.	C
4.	A		14.	D
5.	D		15.	A
6.	D		16.	D
7.	C		17.	B
8.	A		18.	C
9.	D		19.	C
10.	B		20.	B

21.	C
22.	D
23.	D
24.	A
25.	C

EXAMINATION SECTION
TEST 1

DIRECTIONS: Each question or incomplete statement is followed by several suggested answers or completions. Select the one that BEST answers the question or completes the statement. *PRINT THE LETTER OF THE CORRECT ANSWER IN THE SPACE AT THE RIGHT.*

1. To check for the entrance of toxic wastes into a treatment plant, each of the following may be reliably observed as indicators EXCEPT   1.____

    A. changes in color of incoming wastewater
    B. waste recording equipment
    C. odors
    D. bulking of sludge in the clarifier

2. An increase in _____ could cause a demand for more oxygen in an aeration tank.   2.____

    A. inert or inorganic wastes
    B. pH
    C. toxic substances
    D. microorganisms

3. Chlorine may be added for hydrogen sulfide control in the   3.____

    A. collection lines   B. aeration tank
    C. plant effluent   D. trickling filter

4. The range of typical carrying capacities, in gallons per minute, of intermediate pumping stations is   4.____

    A. less than 600   B. 200-700
    C. 100-1,600   D. 700-10,000

5. A low sulfanator injector vacuum reading could be caused by   5.____

    A. missing gasket
    B. high back pressure
    C. high-volume injector flow
    D. wrong orifice

6. Before starting a rotating biological contactor process, each of the following should be checked EXCEPT   6.____

    A. lubrication   B. biomass
    C. clearance   D. tightness

7. The capacity for water or wastewater to neutralize acids is expressed in terms of   7.____

    A. pH   B. oxygen demand
    C. alkalinity   D. acidity

8. Which of the following is NOT one of the available methods for determining stormwater flow for the purpose of storm sewer design?   8.____

A.   Rainfall and runoff correlation studies
B.   Inlet method
C.   Hydrograph method
D.   Outlet method

9.   What is the term for the accumulation of residue that appears on trickling filters and must   9._____
be removed periodically?

   A.   Sludges   B.   Slurries   C.   Slugs   D.   Sloughings

10.   A sludge containing a high number of living organisms is referred to as   10._____

   A.   raw   B.   activated   C.   primary   D.   toxic

11.   Which of the following is NOT a plant location where liquid mixing is commonly prac-   11._____
ticed?

   A.   Ponds
   B.   Hydraulic jumps in open channels
   C.   Pipelines
   D.   Venturi flumes

12.   Which of the following industries releases primarily inorganic wastes in its effluent?   12._____

   A.   Paper   B.   Petroleum
   C.   Gravel washing   D.   Dairy

13.   Which of the following collection system variables could upset a plant's activated sludge   13._____
process?

   A.   Discharge by industrial cleaning operations
   B.   Chlorination of return sludge flows
   C.   Decreases in influent flows
   D.   Recycling of digester supernatant

14.   The second-stage BOD is also referred to as the _____ stage.   14._____

   A.   carbonaceous   B.   pretreatment
   C.   flocculation   D.   nitrification

15.   When organic matter decomposes to form foul-smelling products associated with the   15._____
lack of free oxygen, this condition is known as

   A.   shock loading   B.   septicity
   C.   sloughing   D.   sidestreaming

16.   Which type of bacteria has the HIGHEST optimum temperature for treatment?   16._____

   A.   Mesophilic   B.   Cryophilic
   C.   Thermophilic   D.   Psychrophilic

17.   The COD test   17._____

   A.   estimates the total oxygen consumed
   B.   measures the carbon oxygen demand
   C.   provides results more quickly than the BOD test
   D.   measures only the nitrification oxygen demand

18. Which of the following is NOT considered a major factor that may cause variations in lab   18.____
    test results?

    A. The nature of the material being examined
    B. Testing equipment
    C. Sampling procedures
    D. The quantity of material being examined

19. The treatment process that MOST effectively removes suspended solids from wastewa-   19.____
    ter is

    A. sedimentation   B. flocculation
    C. skimming   D. comminution

20. Which of the following is a thickening alternative in sludge processing?   20.____

    A. Flotation   B. Incineration
    C. Elutriation   D. Wet oxidation

21. The device that continuously adds the flow of wastewater into a plant is the   21.____

    A. aggregate   B. turbidity meter
    C. titrator   D. totalizer

22. Two types of measurement required in connection with the operation of a treatment plant   22.____
    are

    A. effluent and downstream
    B. temperature and dissolved oxygen
    C. in-plant and receiving water
    D. temperature and receiving water

23. You may NOT dispose of excess activated sludge waste from package plants   23.____

    A. at a nearby treatment plant
    B. by anaerobic digestion
    C. by removal by septic tank pumper
    D. by aeration in a holding tank, then deposit in a sanitary landfill

24. What is the term for the combination of activated sludge with raw wastewater in a treat-   24.____
    ment plant?

    A. Median   B. Liquefaction
    C. Effluent   D. Mixed liquor

25. Landfills produce poisonous _____ gas as a byproduct of decomposition.   25.____

    A. methane   B. nitrogen
    C. chlorofluorocarbons   D. argon

KEY (CORRECT ANSWERS)

1.	B	11.	A
2.	D	12.	C
3.	A	13.	A
4.	D	14.	D
5.	B	15.	B
6.	B	16.	C
7.	C	17.	C
8.	D	18.	D
9.	D	19.	B
10.	B	20.	A

21.	D
22.	C
23.	B
24.	D
25.	A

TEST 2

DIRECTIONS: Each question or incomplete statement is followed by several suggested answers or completions. Select the one that BEST answers the question or completes the statement. *PRINT THE LETTER OF THE CORRECT ANSWER IN THE SPACE AT THE RIGHT.*

1. Which of the following types of pumps is a kinetic pump?   1.____

    A. Rotary   B. Piston plunger
    C. Hydraulic ram   D. Blow case

2. What device is used to keep floated solids out of the effluent in dissolved air flotation thickeners?   2.____

    A. Cloth screens   B. Microscreens
    C. Effluent baffles   D. Water sprays

3. The _____ is NOT one of the primary factors affecting the flow of wastewater and sewage in sewers.   3.____

    A. viscosity of the liquid
    B. cross-sectional area of the system conduit
    C. time of day
    D. pipe surface

4. What is the term for washing a digested sludge in the plant effluent?   4.____

    A. Masking   B. Elutriation
    C. Hydrolysis   D. Slaking

5. _____ is NOT an objective in periodically pumping sludge from the primary clarifier to the digester.   5.____

    A. Prevention of pump clogging
    B. Prevention of digester overload
    C. Allowance for thicker sludge pumping
    D. Maintenance of good clarifier conditions

6. The toxic chemical LEAST likely to be encountered by treatment plant operators is(are)   6.____

    A. mercury   B. acids
    C. fluorocarbons   D. bases

7. Which concentration of total dissolved solids, in milligrams per liter, would be the MINIMUM required in order to be considered *strong* in wastewater?   7.____

    A. 250   B. 500   C. 850   D. 1,200

8. What is the term for the treatment process in which a tank or reactor is filled, the water is treated, and the tank is emptied?   8.____

    A. Flocculation   B. Centration
    C. Batch process   D. Pond process

9. The mixing of a compound with water to produce a true chemical reaction is to   9.____

    A. dissolve   B. slake   C. strip   D. hydrate

10. If the difference in elevation between inflow and outflow sewers is greater than 1.5 feet, which device is needed?   10.____

    A. Side weir   B. Drop inlet
    C. Baffles   D. Inlet casting

11. Intermittent releases or discharges of industrial wastes are known as   11.____

    A. slurries   B. slugs   C. splashes   D. stop logs

12. Results from the settleability test of activated sludge solids may be used to   12.____

    A. calculate BOD
    B. determine probable flow rates at which sludges may clog equipment
    C. calculate sludge age
    D. determine ability of solids to separate from liquid in final clarifier

13. The device used to measure the temperature of an effluent is a   13.____

    A. thermometer   B. Bourdon tube
    C. thermocouple   D. pug mill

14. Which source is typically the HEAVIEST contributor of total solids in a service area's wastewater supply?   14.____

    A. Industrial wastes   B. Domestic wash waters
    C. Storm runoff   D. Human biological wastes

15. The term for liquid removed from a settled sludge is   15.____

    A. hydrolyte   B. supernatant
    C. aliquot   D. slurry

16. A unit of wastewater moving through the treatment system without dispersing or mixing with the rest of the wastewater in the system is called   16.____

    A. centration   B. plug flow
    C. putrefaction   D. slugging

17. What is the term for the groups or clumps of bacteria or particles that have clustered together during the treatment process?   17.____

    A. Coagulants   B. Slurries
    C. Floes   D. Slugs

18. The purpose of PRIMARY sedimentation is to remove   18.____

    A. settleable and floatable material
    B. roots, rags, and large debris
    C. suspended and dissolved solids
    D. sand and gravel

19. _____ would NOT cause an increase in effluent coliform levels at a treatment plant.   19.____

    A. Mixing problems
    B. An increase in effluent BOD
    C. Solids accumulation in the contact chamber
    D. High chlorine residual

20. What is the term used to describe bacteria that can live under either aerobic or anaerobic conditions?   20.____

   A. Cultured   B. Agglomerated
   C. Filamentous   D. Facultative

21. Which devices are NOT used during pretreatment?   21.____

   A. Racks   B. Comminutors
   C. Screens   D. Coagulators

22. Through which stage in an activated sludge treatment plant would wastewater pass FIRST?   22.____

   A. Grit chambers   B. Bar racks
   C. Settling tanks   D. Primary sedimentation

23. The inorganic gas LEAST likely to be found around a treatment plant is   23.____

   A. ammonia   B. methane
   C. hydrogen sulfide   D. mercaptans

24. The soils in an effluent disposal on land program may be tested using each of the following procedures EXCEPT   24.____

   A. BOD   B. conductivity
   C. pH   D. cation exchange capacity

25. Which of the following is a conditioning alternative in sludge processing?   25.____

   A. Centrifugation   B. Drying
   C. Composing   D. Elutriation

KEY (CORRECT ANSWERS)

1. C			11. B	
2. C			12. D	
3. C			13. C	
4. B			14. A	
5. A			15. B	
6. C			16. B	
7. C			17. C	
8. C			18. A	
9. B			19. D	
10. B			20. D	

21. D
22. B
23. D
24. A
25. D

EXAMINATION SECTION
TEST 1

DIRECTIONS: Each question or incomplete statement is followed by several suggested answers or completions. Select the one that BEST answers the question or completes the statement. *PRINT THE LETTER OF THE CORRECT ANSWER IN THE SPACE AT THE RIGHT.*

1. To measure the diameter of a replacement pump shaft, a(n) _____ should be used.　　1.____

    A. surveyor's chain　　　　　　　　B. micrometer
    C. metallic tape　　　　　　　　　　D. engineer's scale

2. A _____ is used to bypass storm flow in a combined-sewerage system.　　2.____

    A. drop inlet　　　　　　　　　　　B. side weir
    C. hydraulic jump　　　　　　　　　D. baffle

3. The PRIMARY element in a control system is the　　3.____

    A. transmitter　　　　　　　　　　B. receiver
    C. sensor　　　　　　　　　　　　D. controller

4. The use of water to break down complex substances into simpler ones is called　　4.____

    A. dissolving　　　　　　　　　　　B. hydrolysis
    C. coagulation　　　　　　　　　　D. hydrostasis

5. In its progress through a pumping station, wastewater FIRST passes through a　　5.____

    A. comminutor　　　　　　　　　　B. chlorine room
    C. wet well　　　　　　　　　　　　D. barminutor

6. Which of the following is NOT one of the main operational factors for a barminutor?　　6.____

    A. Amount of debris in wastewater
    B. Number of units in service
    C. Head loss through unit
    D. Removal of floatables

7. Which of the following precautions must be taken before attempting to repair a surface aerator?　　7.____

    A. Shut down aerator
    B. Drain aeration tank
    C. Secure header assembly
    D. Test atmosphere for toxic gases

8. Which of the following source types would MOST likely influence the pH of wastewater?　　8.____

    A. Industrial　　　　　　　　　　　B. Commercial
    C. Agricultural　　　　　　　　　　D. Domestic

9. Each of the following items should be carefully controlled in an activated sludge plant in order to prevent sludge bulking EXCEPT　　9.____

    A. filamentous growth　　　　　　　B. length of aeration time
    C. return sludge rate　　　　　　　D. sludge age

10. Sludge blanket depths may be measured by the use of   10._____

    A. ultrasonic transmitters and receivers
    B. pressure gages
    C. floats connected to cables
    D. bubbler tubes

11. The vertical distance from the normal water surface to the top of the confining wall of a   11._____
pond or tank is called the

    A. freeboard   B. force main
    C. header   D. stop log

12. Suspended solids in the effluent from a trickling filter plant may be caused by   12._____

    A. heavy sloughing from the filters
    B. precipitation of solids in the secondary filter
    C. condensation of effluent on secondary equipment
    D. flotation of solids in the primary clarifier

13. What is MOST often produced during the decomposition of domestic wastes?   13._____

    A. Phenols   B. Oxygen
    C. Hydrogen sulfide   D. Sulfur

14. Air compressor vibration sensing devices are used to measure each of the following   14._____
EXCEPT

    A. flow   B. velocity
    C. acceleration   D. displacement

15. The height or energy of liquids above a certain point is measured in terms of   15._____

    A. discharge rate   B. volume
    C. flow   D. head

16. Factors in the design of sanitary sewers include each of the following EXCEPT   16._____

    A. maximum rate for an entire service area's domestic sewage within a specified time
       period
    B. maximum rates from commercial and industrial areas
    C. infiltration allowance for entire service area
    D. maximum rates from domestic and industrial/commercial sources combined

17. Which of the following could prevent a pump from starting?   17._____

    A. Tripped circuit breakers
    B. Air leaks in suction line
    C. High discharge head
    D. Lack of priming

18. Through which stage would wastewater undergoing chemical-physical treatment pass   18._____
FIRST?

    A. Precipitation   B. Stripping
    C. Flocculation   D. Slaking

19. Which of the following could be considered a normal operating condition for micro-screens?

    A. High flow   B. High pH level
    C. Low pH flow   D. Toxic wastes

    19.____

20. The tank in which sludges are placed in order to allow decomposition is known as the

    A. emulsion   B. dessicator
    C. digester   D. percolator

    20.____

21. The conversion of large solid sludge particles into fine particles that can be dissolved or suspended in water is called

    A. hydrolysis   B. liquefaction
    C. comminution   D. recirculation

    21.____

22. A mixture in which two or more liquid substances are held in suspension is called a(n)

    A. solution   B. electrolyte
    C. emulsion   D. reagent

    22.____

23. What is the term for a mass of sludge containing a highly concentrated population of microorganisms?

    A. Septic   B. Seed
    C. Shock load   D. Slug

    23.____

24. Which of the following forms of nitrogen is LEAST important to the wastewater treatment process?

    A. Nitrate   B. Ammonia   C. Elemental   D. Organic

    24.____

25. What is the term for water leaving a centrifuge after the removal of most solids?

    A. Cation exchange   B. Centration
    C. Flocculation   D. Turbidity

    25.____

KEY (CORRECT ANSWERS)

1.	B		11.	A
2.	B		12.	A
3.	C		13.	C
4.	B		14.	A
5.	C		15.	D
6.	D		16.	D
7.	A		17.	A
8.	A		18.	C
9.	D		19.	D
10.	A		20.	C

21.	B
22.	C
23.	B
24.	C
25.	B

TEST 2

DIRECTIONS: Each question or incomplete statement is followed by several suggested answers or completions. Select the one that BEST answers the question or completes the statement. *PRINT THE LETTER OF THE CORRECT ANSWER IN THE SPACE AT THE RIGHT.*

1. The MOST effective treatment process for destroying or removing bacteria from waste-water is through

   A. activated sludge process
   B. trickling filter
   C. chlorination
   D. sedimentation

   1.____

2. Which of the following tasks is NOT associated with the starting of a comminutor?

   A. Check positioning of inlet and outlet gases
   B. Inspect for frayed cables
   C. Adjust cutter blades
   D. Inspect for lubrication and oil leaks

   2.____

3. One of the objectives of digester mixing is

   A. the use of waste gas to run mixers
   B. adequate cooling throughout digester contents
   C. the release of hydrogen sulfide gas
   D. microorganic inoculation of raw sludge

   3.____

4. Which type of bacteria would give the STRONGEST indication of the possible presence of pathogenic bacteria in waste-water?

   A. Coliform   B. Filamentous
   C. Heterotrophic   D. Facultative

   4.____

5. Cryogenic oxygen plants should be shut down for maintenance every

   A. six months   B. year
   C. two years   D. five years

   5.____

6. At the _____ stage in the biological treatment process, aerobic bacteria uses dissolved oxygen to convert carbon compounds to carbon dioxide.

   A. clarifying   B. carbonaceous
   C. nitrification   D. coagulation

   6.____

7. _____ is NOT an influential factor in the settleability of solids in a clarifier.

   A. Detention time
   B. Flow velocity
   C. The movement of sludge scrapers
   D. Temperature

   7.____

8. Which concentration of total organic carbon, in milligrams per liter, would be considered
moderate in wastewater?

    A. 50   B. 100   C. 200   D. 300

  8.____

9. Which of the following is a volume reduction alternative in sludge processing?

    A. Centrifugation   B. Chemical conditioning
    C. Flotation   D. Drying

  9.____

10. The hydraulic loading for a phosphate stripper depends on the

    A. dissolved oxygen of the activated sludge
    B. pH of wastewater
    C. BOD loading of the unit
    D. ability of the aerobic phosphate stripper to remain aerobic

  10.____

11. The range of typical carrying capacities, in gallons per minute, of package-plant pumping
stations is

    A. less than 600   B. 200-700
    C. 100-1,600   D. 700-10,000

  11.____

12. When a sludge becomes too light and refuses to settle properly in a clarifier, this is
known as

    A. centration   B. precipitation
    C. comminution   D. bulking

  12.____

13. In a wet well, level control systems include each of the following EXCEPT

    A. bubblers   B. hearts   C. floats   D. electrodes

  13.____

14. Which of the following is NOT one of the primary sources of odors in a wastewater treatment plant?

    A. Unwashed grit
    B. The carbon adsorption process
    C. Sludge incinerators
    D. Waste-gas burning

  14.____

15. A chemical property used in the classification of irrigation waters is

    A. pH   B. total dissolved solids
    C. BOD   D. aeration

  15.____

16. Which of the following is NOT a potential use for the dissolved air flotation process?

    A. Solids recovery   B. Coagulation
    C. Wastewater treatment   D. Water recovery

  16.____

17. Each of the following is a principal factor determining the use of pumping stations in sewage collection EXCEPT the

    A. elevation of the area or district to be serviced
    B. location of natural drainage areas in relation to the service area
    C. cost of a pumping station
    D. cost of trunk sewer construction

  17.____

18. Through which stage would wastewater undergoing chemical-physical treatment pass LAST?   18.____

    A. Carbon adsorption   B. Lime recovery
    C. Flocculation   D. Slaking

19. Which of the following practices is NOT included in the maintenance of equipment in package operation plants?   19.____

    A. Changing oil in the speed reducer
    B. Adjusting aeration equipment
    C. Washing tank walls and channels
    D. Inspecting the air-lift pump

20. What chemical solution is capable of neutralizing acids or bases without greatly altering pH?   20.____
A(n)

    A. blank   B. alkaline   C. buffer   D. digester

21. Which of the following types of pumps is a displacement pump?   21.____

    A. Centrifugal   B. Electromagnetic
    C. Peripheral   D. Diaphragm

22. A sludge whose solid portion can be separated from the liquid is referred to as   22.____

    A. anhydrous   B. soluble
    C. hydrolytic   D. dewaterable

23. Which of the following could indicate that a high organic waste load has reached the activated sludge process?   23.____
A(n)

    A. *increase* in DO residual in the aeration tank
    B. *increase* in turbidity in the effluent from the secondary chamber
    C. *decrease* in nutrients in the effluent from the secondary chamber
    D. *decrease* in aeration

24. The term for the clogging of the filtering medium or a microscreen or a vacuum filter is   24.____

    A. corrosion   B. head loss
    C. coagulation   D. blinding

25. Through which stage in an activated sludge treatment plant would wastewater pass LAST?   25.____

    A. Grit chamber
    B. Chlorine contact chamber
    C. Settling tanks
    D. Trickling filters

KEY (CORRECT ANSWERS)

1.	C		11.	B
2.	B		12.	D
3.	D		13.	B
4.	A		14.	B
5.	B		15.	B
6.	B		16.	B
7.	C		17.	C
8.	C		18.	A
9.	D		19.	A
10.	A		20.	C

21.	D
22.	D
23.	B
24.	D
25.	B

———

EXAMINATION SECTION
TEST 1

DIRECTIONS: Each question or incomplete statement is followed by several suggested answers or completions. Select the one that BEST answers the question or completes the statement. *PRINT THE LETTER OF THE CORRECT ANSWER IN THE SPACE AT THE RIGHT.*

1. Which of the following is the MOST likely action a supervisor should take to help establish an effective working relationship with his departmental superiors?   1.____

    A. Delay the implementation of new procedures received from superiors in order to evaluate their appropriateness.
    B. Skip the chain of command whenever he feels that it is to his advantage.
    C. Keep supervisors informed of problems in his area and the steps taken to correct them.
    D. Don't take up superiors' time by discussing anticipated problems but wait until the difficulties occur.

2. Of the following, the action a supervisor could take which would *generally* be MOST conducive to the establishment of an effective working relationship with employees includes   2.____

    A. maintaining impersonal relationships to prevent development of biased actions
    B. treating all employees equally without adjusting for individual differences
    C. continuous observation of employees on the job with insistence on constant improvement
    D. careful planning and scheduling of work for your employees

3. Which of the following procedures is the LEAST likely to establish effective working relationships between employees and supervisors?   3.____

    A. Encouraging *two-way* communication with employees
    B. Periodic discussion with employees regarding their job performance
    C. Ignoring employees' gripes concerning job difficulties
    D. Avoiding personal prejudices in dealing with employees

4. Criticism can be used as a tool to point out the weak areas of a subordinate's work performance.   4.____
   Of the following, the BEST action for a supervisor to take so that his criticism will be accepted is to

    A. focus his criticism on the act instead of on the person
    B. exaggerate the errors in order to motivate the employee to do better
    C. pass judgment quickly and privately without investigating the circumstances of the error
    D. generalize the criticism and not specifically point out the errors in performance

5. In trying to improve the motivation of his subordinates, a supervisor can achieve the BEST results by taking action based upon the assumption that most employees   5.____

    A. have an inherent dislike of work
    B. wish to be closely directed
    C. are more interested in security than in assuming responsibility
    D. will exercise self-direction without coercion

6. When there are conflicts or tensions between top management and lower-level employ-   6.____
ees in any department, the supervisor should FIRST attempt to

   A. represent and enforce the management point of view
   B. act as the representative of the workers to get their ideas across to management
   C. serve as a two-way spokesman, trying to interpret each side to the other
   D. remain neutral, but keep informed of changes in the situation

7. A probationary period for new employees is usually provided in many agencies.   7.____
The MAJOR purpose of such a period is *usually* to

   A. allow a determination of employee's suitability for the position
   B. obtain evidence as to employee's ability to perform in a higher position
   C. conform to requirements that ethnic hiring goals be met for all positions
   D. train the new employee in the duties of the position

8. An effective program of orientation for new employees usually includes all of the follow-   8.____
ing EXCEPT

   A. having the supervisor introduce the new employee to his job, outlining his responsibilities and how to carry them out
   B. permitting the new worker to tour the facility or department so he can observe all
parts of it in action
   C. scheduling meetings for new employees, at which the job requirements are
explained to them and they are given personnel manuals
   D. testing the new worker on his skills and sending him to a centralized in-service
workshop

9. In-service training is an important responsibility of many supervisors.   9.____
The MAJOR reason for such training is to

   A. avoid future grievance procedures because employees might say they were not
prepared to carry out their jobs
   B. maximize the effectiveness of the department by helping each employee perform
at his full potential
   C. satisfy inspection teams from central headquarters of the department
   D. help prevent disagreements with members of the community

10. There are many forms of useful in-service training. Of the following, the training method   10.____
which is NOT an appropriate technique for leadership development is to

   A. provide special workshops or clinics in activity skills
   B. conduct institutes to familiarize new workers with the program of the department
and with their roles
   C. schedule team meetings for problem-solving, including both supervisors and lead-
ers
   D. have the leader rate himself on an evaluation form periodically

11. Of the following techniques of evaluating work training programs, the one that is BEST is to   11.____

    A. pass out a carefully designed questionnaire to the trainees at the completion of the program
    B. test the knowledge that trainees have both at the beginning of training and at its completion
    C. interview the trainees at the completion of the program
    D. evaluate performance before and after training for both a control group and an experimental group

12. Assume that a new supervisor is having difficulty making his instructions to subordinates clearly understood.   12.____
The one of the following which is the FIRST step he should take in dealing with this problem is to

    A. set up a training workshop in communication skills
    B. determine the extent and nature of the communications gap
    C. repeat both verbal and written instructions several times
    D. simplify his written and spoken vocabulary

13. A director has not properly carried out the orders of his assistant supervisor on several occasions to the point where he has been successively warned, reprimanded, and severely reprimanded.   13.____
When the director once again does not carry out orders, the PROPER action for the assistant supervisor to take is to

    A. bring the director up on charges of failing to perform his duties properly
    B. have a serious discussion with the director, explaining the need for the orders and the necessity for carrying them out
    C. recommend that the director be transferred to another district
    D. severely reprimand the director again, making clear that no further deviation will be countenanced

14. A supervisor with several subordinates becomes aware that two of these subordinates are neither friendly nor congenial.   14.____
In making assignments, it would be BEST for the supervisor to

    A. disregard the situation
    B. disregard the situation in making a choice of assignment but emphasize the need for teamwork
    C. investigate the situation to find out who is at fault and give that individual the less desirable assignments until such time as he corrects his attitude
    D. place the unfriendly subordinates in positions where they have as little contact with one another as possible

15. A DESIRABLE characteristic of a good supervisor is that he should   15.____

    A. identify himself with his subordinates rather than with higher management
    B. inform subordinates of forthcoming changes in policies and programs only when they directly affect the subordinates' activities
    C. make advancement of the subordinates contingent on personal loyalty to the supervisor
    D. make promises to subordinates only when sure of the ability to keep them

16. The supervisor who is MOST likely to be successful is the one who   16._____

    A. refrains from exercising the special privileges of his position
    B. maintains a formal attitude toward his subordinates
    C. maintains an informal attitude toward his subordinates
    D. represents the desires of his subordinates to his superiors

17. Application of sound principles of human relations by a supervisor may be expected to   17._____
_____ the need for formal discipline.

    A. decrease   B. have no effect on
    C. increase   D. obviate

18. The MOST important generally approved way to maintain or develop high morale in   18._____
one's subordinates is to

    A. give warnings and reprimands in a jocular manner
    B. excuse from staff conferences those employees who are busy
    C. keep them informed of new developments and policies of higher management
    D. refrain from criticizing their faults directly

19. In training subordinates, an IMPORTANT principle for the supervisor to recognize is that   19._____

    A. a particular method of instruction will be of substantially equal value for all employ-
ees in a given title
    B. it is difficult to train people over 50 years of age because they have little capacity
for learning
    C. persons undergoing the same course of training will learn at different rates of
speed
    D. training can seldom achieve its purpose unless individual instruction is the chief
method used

20. Over an extended period of time, a subordinate is MOST likely to become and remain   20._____
most productive is the supervisor

    A. accords praise to the subordinate whenever his work is satisfactory, withholding
criticism except in the case of very inferior work
    B. avoids both praise and criticism except for outstandingly good or bad work per-
formed by the subordinate
    C. informs the subordinate of his shortcomings, as viewed by management, while
according praise only when highly deserved
    D. keeps the subordinate informed of the degree of satisfaction with which his perfor-
mance of the job is viewed by management

KEY (CORRECT ANSWERS)

1.	C		11.	D
2.	D		12.	B
3.	C		13.	A
4.	A		14.	D
5.	D		15.	D
6.	C		16.	D
7.	A		17.	A
8.	D		18.	C
9.	B		19.	C
10.	D		20.	D

TEST 2

DIRECTIONS: Each question or incomplete statement is followed by several suggested answers or completions. Select the one that BEST answers the question or completes the statement. *PRINT THE LETTER OF THE CORRECT ANSWER IN THE SPACE AT THE RIGHT.*

1. A supervisor has just been told by a subordinate, Mr. Jones, that another employee, Mr. Smith, deliberately disobeyed an important rule of the department by taking home some confidential departmental material.
   Of the following courses of action, it would be MOST advisable for the supervisor first to

   A. discuss the matter privately with both Mr. Jones and Mr. Smith at the same time
   B. call a meeting of the entire staff and discuss the matter generally without mention-ing any employee by name
   C. arrange to supervise Mr. Smith's activities more closely
   D. discuss the matter privately with Mr. Smith

1.____

2. The one of the following actions which would be MOST efficient and economical for a supervisor to take to minimize the effect of periodic fluctuations in the work load of his unit is to

   A. increase his permanent staff until it is large enough to handle the work of the busy loads
   B. request the purchase of time and labor saving equipment to be used primarily dur-ing the busy loads
   C. lower, temporarily, the standards for quality of work performance during peak loads
   D. schedule for the slow periods work that is not essential to perform during the busy periods

2.____

3. Discipline of employees is usually a. supervisor's responsibility. There may be several useful forms of disciplinary action.
   Of the following, the form that is LEAST appropriate is the

   A. written reprimand or warning
   B. involuntary transfer to another work setting
   C. demotion or suspension
   D. assignment of added hours of work each week

3.____

4. Of the following, the MOST effective means of dealing with employee disciplinary prob-lems is to

   A. give personality tests to individuals to identify their psychological problems
   B. distribute and discuss a policy manual containing exact rules governing employee behavior
   C. establish a single, clear penalty to be imposed for all wrongdoing irrespective of degree
   D. have supervisors get to know employees well through social mingling

4.____

5. A recently developed technique for appraising work performance is to have the supervi-   5.____
sor record on a continual basis all significant incidents in each subordinate's behavior
that indicate unsuccessful action and those that indicate poor behavior.
Of the following, a MAJOR disadvantage of this method of performance appraisal is
that it

    A. often leads to overly close supervision
    B. results in competition among those subordinates being evaluated
    C. tends to result in superficial judgments
    D. lacks objectivity for evaluating performance

6. Assume that you are a supervisor and have observed the performance of an employee   6.____
during a period of time. You have concluded that his performance needs improvement.
In order to improve his performance, it would, therefore, be BEST for you to

    A. note your findings in the employee's personnel folder so that his behavior is a mat-
ter of record
    B. report the findings to the personnel officer so he can take prompt action
    C. schedule a problem-solving conference with the employee
    D. recommend his transfer to simpler duties

7. When an employee's absences or latenesses seem to be nearing excessiveness, the   7.____
supervisor should speak with him to find out what the problem is.
Of the following, if such a discussion produces no reasonable explanation, the discussion usually BEST serves to

    A. affirm clearly the supervisor's adherence to proper policy
    B. alert other employees that such behavior is unacceptable
    C. demonstrate that the supervisor truly represents higher management
    D. notify the employee that his behavior is being observed and evaluated

8. Assume that an employee willfully and recklessly violates an important agency regula-   8.____
tion. The nature of the violation is of such magnitude that it demands immediate action,
but the facts of the case are not entirely clear. Further, assume that the supervisor is free
to make any of the following recommendations.
The MOST appropriate action for the supervisor to take is to recommend that the
employee be

    A. discharged   B. suspended
    C. forced to resign   D. transferred

9. Although employees' titles may be identical, each position in that title may be consider-   9.____
ably different.
Of the following, a supervisor should carefully assign each employee to a specific position based PRIMARILY on the employee's

    A. capability   B. experience
    C. education   D. seniority

10. The one of the following situations where it is MOST appropriate to transfer an employee   10.____
to a similar assignment is one in which the employee

    A. lacks motivation and interest
    B. experiences a personality conflict with his supervisor

C. is negligent in the performance of his duties
D. lacks capacity or ability to perform assigned tasks

11. The one of the following which is LEAST likely to be affected by improvements in the morale of personnel is employee　　　　　11.____

    A. skill   B. absenteeism
    C. turnover   D. job satisfaction

12. The one of the following situations in which it is LEAST appropriate for a supervisor to delegate authority to subordinates is where the supervisor　　　　　12.____

    A. lacks confidence in his own abilities to perform certain work
    B. is overburdened and cannot handle all his responsibilities
    C. refers all disciplinary problems to his subordinate
    D. has to deal with an emergency or crisis

13. Assume that it has come to your attention that two of your subordinates have shouted at each other and have almost engaged in a fist fight. Luckily, they were separated by some of the other employees.　　　　　13.____
Of the following, your BEST immediate course of action would *generally* be to

    A. reprimand the senior of the two subordinates since he should have known better
    B. hear the story from both employees and any witnesses and then take needed disciplinary action
    C. ignore the matter since nobody was physically hurt
    D. immediately suspend and fine both employees pending a departmental hearing

14. You have been delegating some of your authority to one of your subordinates because of his leadership potential. Which of the following actions is LEAST conducive to the growth and development of this individual for a supervisory position?　　　　　14.____

    A. Use praise only when it will be effective
    B. Give very detailed instructions and supervise the employee closely to be sure that the instructions are followed precisely
    C. Let the subordinate proceed with his planned course of action even if mistakes, within a permissible range, are made
    D. Intervene on behalf of the subordinate whenever an assignment becomes difficult for him

15. A rumor has been spreading in your department concerning the possibility of layoffs due to decreased revenues.　　　　　15.____
As a supervisor, you should GENERALLY

    A. deny the rumor, whether it is true or false, in order to keep morale from declining
    B. inform the men to the best of your knowledge about this situation and keep them advised of any new information
    C. tell the men to forget about the rumor and concentrate on increasing their productivity
    D. ignore the rumor since it is not authorized information

16. Within an organization, every supervisor should know to whom he reports and who reports to him.
The one of the following which is achieved by use of such structured relationships is

    A. unity of command   B. confidentiality
    C. esprit de corps   D. promotion opportunities

16.____

17. Almost every afternoon, one of your employees comes back from his break ten minutes late without giving you any explanation.
Which of the following actions should you take FIRST in this situation?

    A. Assign the employee to a different type of work and observe whether his behavior changes
    B. Give the employee extra work to do so that he will have to return on time
    C. Ask the employee for an explanation for his lateness
    D. Tell the employee he is jeopardizing the break for everyone

17.____

18. When giving instructions to your employees in a group, which one of the following should you make certain to do?

    A. Speak in a casual, offhand manner
    B. Assume that your employees fully understand the instructions
    C. Write out your instructions beforehand and read them to the employees
    D. Tell exactly who is to do what

18.____

19. A fist fight develops between two men under your supervision.
The MOST advisable course of action for you to take FIRST is to

    A. call the police
    B. have the other workers pull them apart
    C. order them to stop
    D. step between the two men

19.____

20. You have assigned some difficult and unusual work to one of your most experienced and competent subordinates.
If you notice that he is doing the work incorrectly, you should

    A. assign the work to another employee
    B. reprimand him in private
    C. show him immediately how the work should be done
    D. wait until the job is completed and then correct his errors

20.____

KEY (CORRECT ANSWERS)

1. D	11. A
2. D	12. C
3. D	13. B
4. B	14. B
5. A	15. B
6. C	16. A
7. D	17. C
8. B	18. D
9. A	19. C
10. B	20. C

———

PHILOSOPHY, PRINCIPLES, PRACTICES AND TECHNICS
OF
SUPERVISION, ADMINISTRATION, MANAGEMENT AND ORGANIZATION

TABLE OF CONTENTS

TABLE OF CONTENTS (CONTINUED)

PHILOSOPHY, PRINCIPLES, PRACTICES, AND TECHNICS
OF
SUPERVISION, ADMINISTRATION, MANAGEMENT AND ORGANIZATION

I. MEANING OF SUPERVISION

The extension of the democratic philosophy has been accompanied by an extension in the scope of supervision. Modern leaders and supervisors no longer think of supervision in the narrow sense of being confined chiefly to visiting employees, supplying materials, or rating the staff. They regard supervision as being intimately related to all the concerned agencies of society, they speak of the supervisor's function in terms of "growth", rather than the "improvement," of employees.

This modern concept of supervision may be defined as follows:

Supervision is leadership and the development of leadership within groups which are cooperatively engaged in inspection, research, training, guidance and evaluation.

II. THE OLD AND THE NEW SUPERVISION

TRADITIONAL
1. Inspection
2. Focused on the employee
3. Visitation
4. Random and haphazard
5. Imposed and authoritarian
6. One person usually

MODERN
1. Study and analysis
2. Focused on aims, materials, methods, supervisors, employees, environment
3. Demonstrations, intervisitation, workshops, directed reading, bulletins, etc.
4. Definitely organized and planned (scientific)
5. Cooperative and democratic
6. Many persons involved (creative)

III THE EIGHT (8) BASIC PRINCIPLES OF THE NEW SUPERVISION

1. PRINCIPLE OF RESPONSIBILITY
Authority to act and responsibility for acting must be joined.
a. If you give responsibility, give authority.
b. Define employee duties clearly.
c. Protect employees from criticism by others.
d. Recognize the rights as well as obligations of employees.
e. Achieve the aims of a democratic society insofar as it is possible within the area of your work.
f. Establish a situation favorable to training and learning.
g. Accept ultimate responsibility for everything done in your section, unit, office, division, department.
h. Good administration and good supervision are inseparable.

2. *PRINCIPLE OF AUTHORITY*

The success of the supervisor is measured by the extent to which the power of authority is not used.

    a. Exercise simplicity and informality in supervision.

    b. Use the simplest machinery of supervision.

    c. If it is good for the organization as a whole, it is probably justified.

    d. Seldom be arbitrary or authoritative.

    e. Do not base your work on the power of position or of personality.

    f. Permit and encourage the free expression of opinions.

3. *PRINCIPLE OF SELF-GROWTH*

The success of the supervisor is measured by the extent to which, and the speed with which, he is no longer needed.

    a. Base criticism on principles, not on specifics.

    b. Point out higher activities to employees.

    c. Train for self-thinking by employees, to meet new situations.

    d. Stimulate initiative, self-reliance and individual responsibility.

    e. Concentrate on stimulating the growth of employees rather than on removing defects.

4. *PRINCIPLE OF INDIVIDUAL WORTH*

Respect for the individual is a paramount consideration in supervision.

    a. Be human and sympathetic in dealing with employees.

    b. Don't nag about things to be done.

    c. Recognize the individual differences among employees and seek opportunities to permit best expression of each personality.

5. *PRINCIPLE OF CREATIVE LEADERSHIP*

The best supervision is that which is not apparent to the employee.

    a. Stimulate, don't drive employees to creative action.

    b. Emphasize doing good things.

    c. Encourage employees to do what they do best.

    d. Do not be too greatly concerned with details of subject or method.

    e. Do not be concerned exclusively with immediate problems and activities.

    f. Reveal higher activities and make them both desired and maximally possible.

    g. Determine procedures in the light of each situation but see that these are derived from a sound basic philosophy.

    h. Aid, inspire and lead so as to liberate the creative spirit latent in all good employees.

6. *PRINCIPLE OF SUCCESS AND FAILURE*

There are no unsuccessful employees, only unsuccessful supervisors who have failed to give proper leadership.

    a. Adapt suggestions to the capacities, attitudes, and prejudices of employees.

    b. Be gradual, be progressive, be persistent.

    c. Help the employee find the general principle; have the employee apply his own problem to the general principle.

    d. Give adequate appreciation for good work and honest effort.

    e. Anticipate employee difficulties and help to prevent them.

    f. Encourage employees to do the desirable things they will do anyway.

    g. Judge your supervision by the results it secures.

7. *PRINCIPLE OF SCIENCE*

Successful supervision is scientific, objective, and experimental. It is based on facts, not on prejudices.

      a. Be cumulative in results.
      b. Never divorce your suggestions from the goals of training.
      c. Don't be impatient of results.
      d. Keep all matters on a professional, not a personal level.
      e. Do not be concerned exclusively with immediate problems and activities.
      f. Use objective means of determining achievement and rating where possible.

8. *PRINCIPLE OF COOPERATION*

Supervision is a cooperative enterprise between supervisor and employee.

      a. Begin with conditions as they are.
      b. Ask opinions of all involved when formulating policies.
      c. Organization is as good as its weakest link.
      d. Let employees help to determine policies and department programs.
      e. Be approachable and accessible - physically and mentally.
      f. Develop pleasant social relationships.

IV. WHAT IS ADMINISTRATION?

Administration is concerned with providing the environment, the material facilities, and the operational procedures that will promote the maximum growth and development of supervisors and employees. (Organization is an aspect, and a concomitant, of administration.)

There is no sharp line of demarcation between supervision and administration; these functions are intimately interrelated and, often, overlapping. They are complementary activities.

1. *PRACTICES COMMONLY CLASSED AS "SUPERVISORY"*

      a. Conducting employees conferences
      b. Visiting sections, units, offices, divisions, departments
      c. Arranging for demonstrations
      d. Examining plans
      e. Suggesting professional reading
      f. Interpreting bulletins
      g. Recommending in-service training courses
      h. Encouraging experimentation
      i. Appraising employee morale
      j. Providing for intervisitation

2. *PRACTICES COMMONLY CLASSIFIED AS "ADMINISTRATIVE"*

      a. Management of the office
      b. Arrangement of schedules for extra duties
      c. Assignment of rooms or areas
      d. Distribution of supplies
      e. Keeping records and reports
      f. Care of audio-visual materials
      g. Keeping inventory records
      h. Checking record cards and books
      i. Programming special activities
      j. Checking on the attendance and punctuality of employees

3. *PRACTICES COMMONLY CLASSIFIED AS BOTH "SUPERVISORY" AND "ADMINISTRATIVE"*
   a. Program construction
   b. Testing or evaluating outcomes
   c. Personnel accounting
   d. Ordering instructional materials

V. RESPONSIBILITIES OF THE SUPERVISOR

A person employed in a supervisory capacity must constantly be able to improve his own efficiency and ability. He represents the employer to the employees and only continuous self-examination can make him a capable supervisor.

Leadership and training are the supervisor's responsibility. An efficient working unit is one in which the employees work with the supervisor. It is his job to bring out the best in his employees. He must always be relaxed, courteous and calm in his association with his employees. Their feelings are important, and a harsh attitude does not develop the most efficient employees.

VI. COMPETENCIES OF THE SUPERVISOR

1. Complete knowledge of the duties and responsibilities of his position.
2. To be able to organize a job, plan ahead and carry through.
3. To have self-confidence and initiative.
4. To be able to handle the unexpected situation and make quick decisions.
5. To be able to properly train subordinates in the positions they are best suited for.
6. To be able to keep good human relations among his subordinates.
7. To be able to keep good human relations between his subordinates and himself and to earn their respect and trust.

VII. THE PROFESSIONAL SUPERVISOR-EMPLOYEE RELATIONSHIP

There are two kinds of efficiency: one kind is only apparent and is produced in organizations through the exercise of mere discipline; this is but a simulation of the second, or true, efficiency which springs from spontaneous cooperation. If you are a manager, no matter how great or small your responsibility, it is your job, in the final analysis, to create and develop this involuntary cooperation among the people whom you supervise. For, no matter how powerful a combination of money, machines, and materials a company may have, this is a dead and sterile thing without a team of willing, thinking and articulate people to guide it.

The following 21 points are presented as indicative of the exemplary basic relationship that should exist between supervisor and employee:

1. Each person wants to be liked and respected by his fellow employee and wants to be treated with consideration and respect by his superior.
2. The most competent employee will make an error. However, in a unit where good relations exist between the supervisor and his employees, tenseness and fear do not exist. Thus, errors are not hidden or covered up and the efficiency of a unit is not impaired.
3. Subordinates resent rules, regulations, or orders that are unreasonable or unexplained.
4. Subordinates are quick to resent unfairness, harshness, injustices and favoritism.
5. An employee will accept responsibility if he knows that he will be complimented for a job well done, and not too harshly chastised for failure; that his supervisor will check the cause of the failure, and, if it was the supervisor's fault, he will assume the blame therefore. If it was the employee's fault, his supervisor will explain the correct method or means of handling the responsibility.

6. An employee wants to receive credit for a suggestion he has made, that is used. If a suggestion cannot be used, the employee is entitled to an explanation. The supervisor should not say "no" and close the subject.
7. Fear and worry slow up a worker's ability. Poor working environment can impair his physical and mental health. A good supervisor avoids forceful methods, threats and arguments to get a job done.
8. A forceful supervisor is able to train his employees individually and as a team, and is able to motivate them in the proper channels.
9. A mature supervisor is able to properly evaluate his subordinates and to keep them happy and satisfied.
10. A sensitive supervisor will never patronize his subordinates.
11. A worthy supervisor will respect his employees' confidences.
12. Definite and clear-cut responsibilities should be assigned to each executive.
13. Responsibility should always be coupled with corresponding authority.
14. No change should be made in the scope or responsibilities of a position without a definite understanding to that effect on the part of all persons concerned.
15. No executive or employee, occupying a single position in the organization, should be subject to definite orders from more than one source.
16. Orders should never be given to subordinates over the head of a responsible executive. Rather than do this, the officer in question should be supplanted.
17. Criticisms of subordinates should, whoever possible, be made privately, and in no case should a subordinate be criticized in the presence of executives or employees of equal or lower rank.
18. No dispute or difference between executives or employees as to authority or responsibilities should be considered too trivial for prompt and careful adjudication.
19. Promotions, wage changes, and disciplinary action should always be approved by the executive immediately superior to the one directly responsible.
20. No executive or employee should ever be required, or expected, to be at the same time an assistant to, and critic of, another.
21. Any executive whose work is subject to regular inspection should, whever practicable, be given the assistance and facilities necessary to enable him to maintain an independent check of the quality of his work.

VIII. MINI-TEXT IN SUPERVISION, ADMINISTRATION, MANAGEMENT, AND ORGANIZATION

A. BRIEF HIGHLIGHTS

Listed concisely and sequentially are major headings and important data in the field for quick recall and review.

1. *LEVELS OF MANAGEMENT*
Any organization of some size has several levels of management. In terms of a ladder the levels are:

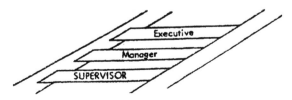

The first level is very important because it is the beginning point of management leadership.

2. *WHAT THE SUPERVISOR MUST LEARN*
A supervisor must learn to:
- (1) Deal with people and their differences
- (2) Get the job done through people
- (3) Recognize the problems when they exist
- (4) Overcome obstacles to good performance
- (5) Evaluate the performance of people
- (6) Check his own performance in terms of accomplishment

3. *A DEFINITION OF SUPERVISOR*
The term supervisor means any individual having authority, in the interests of the employer, to hire, transfer, suspend, lay-off, recall, promote, discharge, assign, reward, or discipline other employees or responsibility to direct them, or to adjust their grievances, or effectively to recommend such action, if, in connection with the foregoing, exercise of such authority is not of a merely routine or clerical nature but requires the use of independent judgment.

4. *ELEMENTS OF THE TEAM CONCEPT*
What is involved in teamwork? The component parts are:
- (1) Members
- (2) A leader
- (3) Goals
- (4) Plans
- (5) Cooperation
- (6) Spirit

5. *PRINCIPLES OF ORGANIZATION*
- (1) A team member must know what his job is.
- (2) Be sure that the nature and scope of a job are understood.
- (3) Authority and responsibility should be carefully spelled out.
- (4) A supervisor should be permitted to make the maximum number of decisions affecting his employees.
- (5) Employees should report to only one supervisor.
- (6) A supervisor should direct only as many employees as he can handle effectively.
- (7) An organization plan should be flexible.
- (8) Inspection and performance of work should be separate.
- (9) Organizational problems should receive immediate attention.
- (10) Assign work in line with ability and experience.

6. *THE FOUR IMPORTANT PARTS OF EVERY JOB*
- (1) Inherent in every job is the *accountability* for results.
- (2) A second set of factors in every job is *responsibilities*.
- (3) Along with duties and responsibilities one must have the *authority* to act within certain limits without obtaining permission to proceed.
- (4) No job exists in a vacuum. The supervisor is surrounded by key *relationships*.

7. *PRINCIPLES OF DELEGATION*
Where work is delegated for the first time, the supervisor should think in terms of these questions:
- (1) Who is best qualified to do this?
- (2) Can an employee improve his abilities by doing this?
- (3) How long should an employee spend on this?
- (4) Are there any special problems for which he will need guidance?
- (5) How broad a delegation can I make?

8. PRINCIPLES OF EFFECTIVE COMMUNICATIONS
(1) Determine the media
(2) To whom directed?
(3) Identification and source authority
(4) Is communication understood?

9. PRINCIPLES OF WORK IMPROVEMENT
(1) Most people usually do only the work which is assigned to them
(2) Workers are likely to fit assigned work into the time available to perform it
(3) A good workload usually stimulates output
(4) People usually do their best work when they know that results will be reviewed or inspected
(5) Employees usually feel that someone else is responsible for conditions of work, workplace layout, job methods, type of tools/equipment, and other such factors
(6) Employees are usually defensive about their job security
(7) Employees have natural resistance to change
(8) Employees can support or destroy a supervisor
(9) A supervisor usually earns the respect of his people through his personal example of diligence and efficiency

10. AREAS OF JOB IMPROVEMENT
The areas of job improvement are quite numerous, but the most common ones which a supervisor can identify and utilize are:

(1) Departmental layout
(2) Flow of work
(3) Workplace layout
(4) Utilization of manpower
(5) Work methods
(6) Materials handling
(7) Utilization
(8) Motion economy

11. SEVEN KEY POINTS IN MAKING IMPROVEMENTS
(1) Select the job to be improved
(2) Study how it is being done now
(3) Question the present method
(4) Determine actions to be taken
(5) Chart proposed method
(6) Get approval and apply
(7) Solicit worker participation

12. CORRECTIVE TECHNIQUES OF JOB IMPROVEMENT

Specific Problems	General Improvement	Corrective Techniques
(1) Size of workload	(1) Departmental layout	(1) Study with scale model
(2) Inability to meet schedules	(2) Flow of work	(2) Flow chart study
(3) Strain and fatigue	(3) Work plan layout	(3) Motion analysis
(4) Improper use of men and skills	(4) Utilization of manpower	(4) Comparison of units produced to standard allowance
(5) Waste, poor quality, unsafe conditions	(5) Work methods	(5) Methods analysis
(6) Bottleneck conditions that hinder output	(6) Materials handling	(6) Flow chart & equipment study
(7) Poor utilization of equipment and machine	(7) Utilization of equipment	(7) Down time vs. running time
(8) Efficiency and productivity of labor	(8) Motion economy	(8) Motion analysis

13. A PLANNING CHECKLIST

(1) Objectives	(6) Resources	(11) Safety
(2) Controls	(7) Manpower	(12) Money
(3) Delegations	(8) Equipment	(13) Work
(4) Communications	(9) Supplies and materials	(14) Timing of improvements
(5) Resources	(10) Utilization of time	

14. FIVE CHARACTERISTICS OF GOOD DIRECTIONS

In order to get results, directions must be:

(1) Possible of accomplishment	(3) Related to mission	(5) Unmistakably clear
(2) Agreeable with worker interests	(4) Planned and complete	

15. TYPES OF DIRECTIONS

(1) Demands or direct orders	(3) Suggestion or implication
(2) Requests	(4) Volunteering

16. CONTROLS

A typical listing of the overall areas in which the supervisor should establish controls might be:

(1) Manpower	(3) Quality of work	(5) Time	(7) Money
(2) Materials	(4) Quantity of work	(6) Space	(8) Methods

17. ORIENTING THE NEW EMPLOYEE

(1) Prepare for him	(3) Orientation for the job
(2) Welcome the new employee	(4) Follow-up

18. CHECKLIST FOR ORIENTING NEW EMPLOYEES

	Yes	No
(1) Do your appreciate the feelings of new employees when they first report for work?	____	____
(2) Are you aware of the fact that the new employee must make a big adjustment to his job?	____	____
(3) Have you given him good reasons for liking the job and the organization?	____	____
(4) Have you prepared for his first day on the job?		
(5) Did you welcome him cordially and make him feel needed?		
(6) Did you establish rapport with him so that he feels free to talk and discuss matters with you?	____	____
(7) Did you explain his job to him and his relationship to you?	____	____
(8) Does he know that his work will be evaluated periodically on a basis that is fair and objective?	____	____
(9) Did you introduce him to his fellow workers in such a way that they are likely to accept him?	____	____
(10) Does he know what employee benefits he will receive?		
(11) Does he understand the importance of being on the job and what to do if he must leave his duty station?	____	____
(12) Has he been impressed with the importance of accident prevention and safe practice?	____	____
(13) Does he generally know his way around the department?	____	____
(14) Is he under the guidance of a sponsor who will teach the right ways of doing things?	____	____
(15) Do you plan to follow-up so that he will continue to adjust successfully to his job?	____	____

19. *PRINCIPLES OF LEARNING*
  (1) Motivation   (2) Demonstration or explanation   (3) Practice

20. *CAUSES OF POOR PERFORMANCE*
  (1) Improper training for job
  (2) Wrong tools
  (3) Inadequate directions
  (4) Lack of supervisory follow-up
  (5) Poor communications
  (6) Lack of standards of performance
  (7) Wrong work habits
  (8) Low morale
  (9) Other

21. *FOUR MAJOR STEPS IN ON-THE-JOB INSTRUCTION*
  (1) Prepare the worker
  (2) Present the operation
  (3) Tryout performance
  (4) Follow-up

22. *EMPLOYEES WANT FIVE THINGS*
  (1) Security (2) Opportunity (3) Recognition (4) Inclusion (5) Expression

23. *SOME DON'TS IN REGARD TO PRAISE*
  (1) Don't praise a person for something he hasn't done
  (2) Don't praise a person unless you can be sincere
  (3) Don't be sparing in praise just because your superior withholds it from you
  (4) Don't let too much time elapse between good performance and recognition of it

24. *HOW TO GAIN YOUR WORKERS' CONFIDENCE*
  Methods of developing confidence include such things as:
  (1) Knowing the interests, habits, hobbies of employees
  (2) Admitting your own inadequacies
  (3) Sharing and telling of confidence in others
  (4) Supporting people when they are in trouble
  (5) Delegating matters that can be well handled
  (6) Being frank and straightforward about problems and working conditions
  (7) Encouraging others to bring their problems to you
  (8) Taking action on problems which impede worker progress

25. *SOURCES OF EMPLOYEE PROBLEMS*
  On-the-job causes might be such things as:
  (1) A feeling that favoritism is exercised in assignments
  (2) Assignment of overtime
  (3) An undue amount of supervision
  (4) Changing methods or systems
  (5) Stealing of ideas or trade secrets
  (6) Lack of interest in job
  (7) Threat of reduction in force
  (8) Ignorance or lack of communications
  (9) Poor equipment
  (10) Lack of knowing how supervisor feels toward employee
  (11) Shift assignments

  Off-the-job problems might have to do with:
  (1) Health   (2) Finances   (3) Housing   (4) Family

26. *THE SUPERVISOR'S KEY TO DISCIPLINE*
There are several key points about discipline which the supervisor should keep in mind:
(1) Job discipline is one of the disciplines of life and is directed by the supervisor.
(2) It is more important to correct an employee fault than to fix blame for it.
(3) Employee performance is affected by problems both on the job and off.
(4) Sudden or abrupt changes in behavior can be indications of important employee problems.
(5) Problems should be dealt with as soon as possible after they are identified.
(6) The attitude of the supervisor may have more to do with solving problems than the techniques of problem solving.
(7) Correction of employee behavior should be resorted to only after the supervisor is sure that training or counseling will not be helpful.
(8) Be sure to document your disciplinary actions.
(9) Make sure that you are disciplining on the basis of facts rather than personal feelings.
(10) Take each disciplinary step in order, being careful not to make snap judgments, or decisions based on impatience.

27. *FIVE IMPORTANT PROCESSES OF MANAGEMENT*
(1) Planning   (2) Organizing   (3) Scheduling
(4) Controlling   (5) Motivating

28. *WHEN THE SUPERVISOR FAILS TO PLAN*
(1) Supervisor creates impression of not knowing his job
(2) May lead to excessive overtime
(3) Job runs itself -- supervisor lacks control
(4) Deadlines and appointments missed
(5) Parts of the work go undone
(6) Work interrupted by emergencies
(7) Sets a bad example
(8) Uneven workload creates peaks and valleys
(9) Too much time on minor details at expense of more important tasks

29. *FOURTEEN GENERAL PRINCIPLES OF MANAGEMENT*
(1) Division of work
(2) Authority and responsibility
(3) Discipline
(4) Unity of command
(5) Unity of direction
(6) Subordination of individual interest to general interest
(7) Remuneration of personnel
(8) Centralization
(9) Scalar chain
(10) Order
(11) Equity
(12) Stability of tenure of personnel
(13) Initiative
(14) Esprit de corps

30. *CHANGE*
Bringing about change is perhaps attempted more often, and yet less well understood, than anything else the supervisor does. How do people generally react to change? (People tend to resist change that is imposed upon them by other individuals or circumstances.

Change is characteristic of every situation. It is a part of every real endeavor where the efforts of people are concerned.

A. Why do people resist change?
   People may resist change because of:
   (1) Fear of the unknown
   (2) Implied criticism
   (3) Unpleasant experiences in the past
   (4) Fear of loss of status
   (5) Threat to the ego
   (6) Fear of loss of economic stability

B. How can we best overcome the resistance to change?
   In initiating change, take these steps:
   (1) Get ready to sell
   (2) Identify sources of help
   (3) Anticipate objections
   (4) Sell benefits
   (5) Listen in depth
   (6) Follow up

B. BRIEF TOPICAL SUMMARIES

I. WHO/WHAT IS THE SUPERVISOR?
1. The supervisor is often called the "highest level employee and the lowest level manager."
2. A supervisor is a member of both management and the work group. He acts as a bridge between the two.
3. Most problems in supervision are in the area of human relations, or people problems.
4. Employees expect: Respect, opportunity to learn and to advance, and a sense of belonging, and so forth.
5. Supervisors are responsible for directing people and organizing work. Planning is of paramount importance.
6. A position description is a set of duties and responsibilities inherent to a given position.
7. It is important to keep the position description up-to-date and to provide each employee with his own copy.

II. THE SOCIOLOGY OF WORK
1. People are alike in many ways; however, each individual is unique.
2. The supervisor is challenged in getting to know employee differences. Acquiring skills in evaluating individuals is an asset.
3. Maintaining meaningful working relationships in the organization is of great importance.
4. The supervisor has an obligation to help individuals to develop to their fullest potential.
5. Job rotation on a planned basis helps to build versatility and to maintain interest and enthusiasm in work groups.
6. Cross training (job rotation) provides backup skills.
7. The supervisor can help reduce tension by maintaining a sense of humor, providing guidance to employees, and by making reasonable and timely decisions. Employees respond favorably to working under reasonably predictable circumstances.
8. Change is characteristic of all managerial behavior. The supervisor must adjust to changes in procedures, new methods, technological changes, and to a number of new and sometimes challenging situations.
9. To overcome the natural tendency for people to resist change, the supervisor should become more skillful in initiating change.

III. PRINCIPLES AND PRACTICES OF SUPERVISION

1. Employees should be required to answer to only one superior.
2. A supervisor can effectively direct only a limited number of employees, depending upon the complexity, variety, and proximity of the jobs involved.
3. The organizational chart presents the organization in graphic form. It reflects lines of authority and responsibility as well as interrelationships of units within the organization.
4. Distribution of work can be improved through an analysis using the "Work Distribution Chart."
5. The "Work Distribution Chart" reflects the division of work within a unit in understandable form.
6. When related tasks are given to an employee, he has a better chance of increasing his skills through training.
7. The individual who is given the responsibility for tasks must also be given the appropriate authority to insure adequate results.
8. The supervisor should delegate repetitive, routine work. Preparation of recurring reports, maintaining leave and attendance records are some examples.
9. Good discipline is essential to good task performance. Discipline is reflected in the actions of employees on the job in the absence of supervision.
10. Disciplinary action may have to be taken when the positive aspects of discipline have failed. Reprimand, warning, and suspension are examples of disciplinary action.
11. If a situation calls for a reprimand, be sure it is deserved and remember it is to be done in private.

IV. DYNAMIC LEADERSHIP

1. A style is a personal method or manner of exerting influence.
2. Authoritarian leaders often see themselves as the source of power and authority.
3. The democratic leader often perceives the group as the source of authority and power.
4. Supervisors tend to do better when using the pattern of leadership that is most natural for them.
5. Social scientists suggest that the effective supervisor use the leadership style that best fits the problem or circumstances involved.
6. All four styles -- telling, selling, consulting, joining -- have their place. Using one does not preclude using the other at another time.
7. The theory X point of view assumes that the average person dislikes work, will avoid it whenever possible, and must be coerced to achieve organizational objectives.
8. The theory Y point of view assumes that the average person considers work to be as natural as play, and, when the individual is committed, he requires little supervision or direction to accomplish desired objectives.
9. The leader's basic assumptions concerning human behavior and human nature affect his actions, decisions, and other managerial practices.
10. Dissatisfaction among employees is often present, but difficult to isolate. The supervisor should seek to weaken dissatisfaction by keeping promises, being sincere and considerate, keeping employees informed, and so forth.
11. Constructive suggestions should be encouraged during the natural progress of the work.

V. PROCESSES FOR SOLVING PROBLEMS

1. People find their daily tasks more meaningful and satisfying when they can improve them.
2. The causes of problems, or the key factors, are often hidden in the background. Ability to solve problems often involves the ability to isolate them from their backgrounds. There is some substance to the cliché that some persons "can't see the forest for the trees."
3. New procedures are often developed from old ones. Problems should be broken down into manageable parts. New ideas can be adapted from old ones.

4. People think differently in problem-solving situations. Using a logical, patterned approach is often useful. One approach found to be useful includes these steps:

    (a) Define the problem   (d) Weigh and decide

    (b) Establish objectives   (e) Take action

    (c) Get the facts   (f) Evaluate action

VI. TRAINING FOR RESULTS

1. Participants respond best when they feel training is important to them.
2. The supervisor has responsibility for the training and development of those who report to him.
3. When training is delegated to others, great care must be exercised to insure the trainer has knowledge, aptitude, and interest for his work as a trainer.
4. Training (learning) of some type goes on continually. The most successful supervisor makes certain the learning contributes in a productive manner to operational goals.
5. New employees are particularly susceptible to training. Older employees facing new job situations require specific training, as well as having need for development and growth opportunities.
6. Training needs require continuous monitoring.
7. The training officer of an agency is a professional with a responsibility to assist supervisors in solving training problems.
8. Many of the self-development steps important to the supervisor's own growth are equally important to the development of peers and subordinates. Knowledge of these is important when the supervisor consults with others on development and growth opportunities.

VII. HEALTH, SAFETY, AND ACCIDENT PREVENTION

1. Management-minded supervisors take appropriate measures to assist employees in maintaining health and in assuring safe practices in the work environment.
2. Effective safety training and practices help to avoid injury and accidents.
3. Safety should be a management goal. All infractions of safety which are observed should be corrected without exception.
4. Employees' safety attitude, training and instruction, provision of safe tools and equipment, supervision, and leadership are considered highly important factors which contribute to safety and which can be influenced directly by supervisors.
5. When accidents do occur they should be investigated promptly for very important reasons, including the fact that information which is gained can be used to prevent accidents in the future.

VIII. EQUAL EMPLOYMENT OPPORTUNITY

1. The supervisor should endeavor to treat all employees fairly, without regard to religion, race, sex, or national origin.
2. Groups tend to reflect the attitude of the leader. Prejudice can be detected even in very subtle form. Supervisors must strive to create a feeling of mutual respect and confidence in every employee.
3. Complete utilization of all human resources is a national goal. Equitable consideration should be accorded women in the work force, minority-group members, the physically and mentally handicapped, and the older employee. The important question is: "Who can do the job?"
4. Training opportunities, recognition for performance, overtime assignments, promotional opportunities, and all other personnel actions are to be handled on an equitable basis.

IX. IMPROVING COMMUNICATIONS

1. Communications is achieving understanding between the sender and the receiver of a message. It also means sharing information -- the creation of understanding.
2. Communication is basic to all human activity. Words are means of conveying meanings; however, real meanings are in people.
3. There are very practical differences in the effectiveness of one-way, impersonal, and two-way communications. Words spoken face-to-face are better understood. Telephone conversations are effective, but lack the rapport of person-to-person exchanges. The whole person communicates.
4. Cooperation and communication in an organization go hand in hand. When there is a mutual respect between people, spelling out rules and procedures for communicating is unnecessary.
5. There are several barriers to effective communications. These include failure to listen with respect and understanding, lack of skill in feedback, and misinterpreting the meanings of words used by the speaker. It is also common practice to listen to what we want to hear, and tune out things we do not want to hear.
6. Communication is management's chief problem. The supervisor should accept the challenge to communicate more effectively and to improve interagency and intra-agency communications.
7. The supervisor may often plan for and conduct meetings. The planning phase is critical and may determine the success or the failure of a meeting.
8. Speaking before groups usually requires extra effort. Stage fright may never disappear completely, but it can be controlled.

X. SELF-DEVELOPMENT

1. Every employee is responsible for his own self-development.
2. Toastmaster and toastmistress clubs offer opportunities to improve skills in oral communications.
3. Planning for one's own self-development is of vital importance. Supervisors know their own strengths and limitations better than anyone else.
4. Many opportunities are open to aid the supervisor in his developmental efforts, including job assignments; training opportunities, both governmental and non-governmental -- to include universities and professional conferences and seminars.
5. Programmed instruction offers a means of studying at one's own rate.
6. Where difficulties may arise from a supervisor's being away from his work for training, he may participate in televised home study or correspondence courses to meet his self-develop- ment needs.

XI. TEACHING AND TRAINING

A. The Teaching Process

Teaching is encouraging and guiding the learning activities of students toward established goals. In most cases this process consists in five steps: preparation, presentation, summarization, evaluation, and application.

1. Preparation
Preparation is twofold in nature; that of the supervisor and the employee.
Preparation by the supervisor is absolutely essential to success. He must know what, when, where, how, and whom he will teach. Some of the factors that should be considered are:

(1) The objectives	(5) Employee interest
(2) The materials needed	(6) Training aids
(3) The methods to be used	(7) Evaluation
(4) Employee participation	(8) Summarization

Employee preparation consists in preparing the employee to receive the material. Probably the most important single factor in the preparation of the employee is arousing and maintaining his interest. He must know the objectives of the training, why he is there, how the material can be used, and its importance to him.

2. Presentation

In presentation, have a carefully designed plan and follow it.
The plan should be accurate and complete, yet flexible enough to meet situations as they arise. The method of presentation will be determined by the particular situation and objectives.

3. Summary

A summary should be made at the end of every training unit and program. In addition, there may be internal summaries depending on the nature of the material being taught. The important thing is that the trainee must always be able to understand how each part of the new material relates to the whole.

4. Application

The supervisor must arrange work so the employee will be given a chance to apply new knowledge or skills while the material is still clear in his mind and interest is high. The trainee does not really know whether he has learned the material until he has been given a chance to apply it. If the material is not applied, it loses most of its value.

5. Evaluation

The purpose of all training is to promote learning. To determine whether the training has been a success or failure, the supervisor must evaluate this learning.

In the broadest sense evaluation includes all the devices, methods, skills, and techniques used by the supervisor to keep him self and the employees informed as to their progress toward the objectives they are pursuing. The extent to which the employee has mastered the knowledge, skills, and abilities, or changed his attitudes, as determined by the program objectives, is the extent to which instruction has succeeded or failed.

Evaluation should not be confined to the end of the lesson, day, or program but should be used continuously. We shall note later the way this relates to the rest of the teaching process.

B. Teaching Methods

A teaching method is a pattern of identifiable student and instructor activity used in presenting training material.

All supervisors are faced with the problem of deciding which method should be used at a given time.

As with all methods, there are certain advantages and disadvantages to each method.

1. Lecture

The lecture is direct oral presentation of material by the supervisor. The present trend is to place less emphasis on the trainer's activity and more on that of the trainee.

2. Discussion

Teaching by discussion or conference involves using questions and other techniques to arouse interest and focus attention upon certain areas, and by doing so creating a learning situation. This can be one of the most valuable methods because it gives the employees 'an opportunity to express their ideas and pool their knowledge.

3. Demonstration

The demonstration is used to teach how something works or how to do something. It can be used to show a principle or what the results of a series of actions will be. A well-staged demonstration is particularly effective because it shows proper methods of performance in a realistic manner.

4. Performance

Performance is one of the most fundamental of all learning techniques or teaching methods. The trainee may be able to tell how a specific operation should be performed but he cannot be sure he knows how to perform the operation until he has done so.

5. Which Method to Use

Moreover, there are other methods and techniques of teaching. It is difficult to use any method without other methods entering into it. In any learning situation a combination of methods is usually more effective than anyone method alone.

Finally, evaluation must be integrated into the other aspects of the teaching-learning process.

It must be used in the motivation of the trainees; it must be used to assist in developing understanding during the training; and it must be related to employee application of the results of training.

This is distinctly the role of the supervisor.

BASIC FUNDAMENTALS OF WATER POLLUTION

TABLE OF CONTENTS

BASIC FUNDAMENTALS OF WATER POLLUTION

COLLECTING AND TREATING WASTES

The most common form of pollution control in the United States consists of a system of sewers and waste treatment plants. The sewers collect the waste water from homes, businesses, and many industries and deliver it to the plants for treatment to make it fit for discharge into streams or for reuse.

There are two kinds of sewer systems — combined and separate. Combined sewers carry away both water polluted by human use and water polluted as it drains off homes, streets, or land during a storm.

In a separated system, one system of sewers, usually called sanitary, carries only sewage. Another system of storm sewers takes care of the large volumes of water from rain or melting snow.

Each home has a sewer or pipe which connects to the common or lateral sewer beneath a nearby street. Lateral sewers connect with larger sewers called trunk or main sewers. In a combined sewer system, these trunk or main sewers discharge into a larger sewer called an interceptor. The interceptor is designed to carry several times the dry-weather flow of the system feeding into it.

During dry weather when the sewers are handling only the normal amount of waste water, all of it is carried to the waste treatment plant. During a storm when the amount of water in the sewer system is much greater, part of the water, including varying amounts of raw sewage, is allowed to bypass directly into the receiving streams. The rest of the wastes are sent to the treatment plant. If part of the increased load of water were not diverted, the waste treatment plant would be overloaded and the purifying processes would not function properly. (A research, development, and demonstration program is being conducted to solve this urban runoff pollution problem. The aim is to develop technology that will control and/or treat combined sewer overflows, storm water discharges, and general washoff of rainwater polluted by dirt or other contaminants on the land.)

Interceptor sewers are also used in sanitary sewer systems as collectors of flow from main sewers and trunks, but do not normally include provisions for bypassing.

A waste treatment plant's basic function is to speed up the natural processes by which water purifies itself. In many cases, nature's treatment process in streams and lakes was adequate before our population and industry grew to their present size.

When the sewage of previous years was dumped into waterways, the natural process of purification began. First, the sheer volume of clean water in the stream diluted the small amount of wastes. Bacteria and other small organisms in the water consumed the sewage or other organic matter, turning it into new bacterial cells, carbon dioxide, and other products.

But the bacteria normally present in water must have oxygen to do their part in breaking down the sewage. Water acquires this all important oxygen by absorbing it from the air and from plants that grow in the water itself. These plants use sunlight to turn the carbon dioxide present in water into oxygen.

The life and death of any body of water depend mainly upon its ability to maintain a certain amount of dissolved oxygen. This dissolved oxygen — or DO — is what fish breathe. Without it, they suffocate. If only a small amount of sewage is dumped into a stream, fish are not affected, and the bacteria can do their work and the stream can quickly restore its oxygen loss from the atmosphere and from plants. Trouble begins when the sewage load is excessive. The sewage will decay and the water will begin to give off odors. If carried to the extreme, the water could lose all of its oxygen, resulting in the death of fish and beneficial plant life.

Since dissolved oxygen is the key element in the life of water, the demands on it are used as a measure in telling how well a sewage treatment plant is working. This measuring device is called biochemical oxygen demand, or BOD. If the effluent or the end-product from a treatment plant has a high content of organic pollutants, the effluent will have a high BOD. In other words, it will demand more oxygen from the water to break down the sewage and consequently will leave the water with less oxygen (and also dirtier).

With the growth of the nation, the problems of pollution have become more complex. The increased amounts of wastes and the larger demands for water have reduced the capacity of running water to purify itself. Consequently, cities and industry have had to begin thinking about removing as much as possible of the oxygen-demanding pollutants from their sewage.

Adequate treatment of wastes along with providing a sufficient supply of clean water has become a major concern.

Primary Treatment

At present, there are two basic ways of treating wastes. They are called primary and secondary. In primary treatment, solids are allowed to settle and are removed from the water Secondary treatment, a further step in purifying waste water, uses biological processes.

As sewage enters a plant for primary treatment, it flows through a screen. The screen removes large floating objects such as rags and sticks that may clog pumps and small pipes. The screens vary from coarse to fine — from those with parallel steel or iron bars with openings of about half an inch or more to screens with much smaller openings.

Screens are generally placed in a chamber or channel in an inclined position to the flow of the sewage to make cleaning easier. The debris caught on the upstream surface of the screen can be raked off manually or mechanically.

Some plants use a device known as a comminutor which combines the functions of a screen and a grinder. These devices catch and then cut or shred the heavy solid material. In the process, the pulverized matter remains in the sewage flow to be removed later in a settling tank.

After the sewage has been screened, it passes into what is called a grit chamber where sand, grit, cinders, and small stones are allowed to settle to the bottom. A grit chamber is highly important for cities with combined sewer systems because it will remove the grit or gravel that washes off streets or land during a storm and ends up at treatment plants.

The unwanted grit or gravel from this process is usually disposed of by filling land near a treatment plant.

In some plants, another screen is placed after the grit chamber to remove any further material that might damage equipment or interfere with later processes.

With the screening completed and the grit removed, the sewage still contains dissolved organic and inorganic matter along with suspended solids. The latter consist of minute particles of matter that can be removed from the sewage by treatment in a sedimentation tank. When the speed of the flow of sewage through one of these tanks is reduced, the suspended solids will gradually sink to the bottom. This mass of solids is called raw sludge.

Various methods have been devised for removing sludge from the tanks.

In older plants, sludge removal was done by hand. After a tank had been in service for several days or weeks, the sewage flow was diverted to another tank. The sludge in the bottom of the out-of-service tank was pushed or flushed with water to a pit near the tank and then removed, usually by pumping, for further treatment or disposal.

Almost all plants built within the past 30 years have had a mechanical means for removing the sludge from sedimentation tanks. Some plants remove it continuously while others remove it at intervals.

To complete the primary treatment, the effluent from the sedimentation tank is chlorinated before being discharged into a stream or river. Chlorine gas is fed into the water to kill and reduce the number of disease-causing bacteria. Chlorination also helps to reduce objectionable odors.

Although 30 percent of the municipalities in the United States give only primary treatment to their sewage, this process by itself is considered entirely inadequate for most needs.

Today's cities and industry, faced with increased amounts of wastes and wastes that are more difficult to remove from water, have turned to secondary and even advanced waste treatment.

Secondary Treatment

Secondary treatment removes up to 90 percent of the organic matter in sewage by making use of the bacteria in it. The two principal types of secondary treatment are trickling filters and the activated-sludge process.

The trickling filter process or the activated-sludge process is used mostly today. After the effluent leaves the sedimentation tank in the primary stage of treatment, it flows or is pumped to a facility using one or the other of these processes. A trickling filter is simply a bed of stones from three to ten feet deep through which the sewage passes. Bacteria gather and multiply on these stones until they can consume most of the organic matter in the sewage. The cleaner water trickles out through pipes in the bottom of the filter for further treatment.

The sewage is applied to the bed of stones in two principal ways. One method consists of distributing the effluent intermittently through a network of pipes laid on or beneath the surface of the stones.

Attached to these pipes are smaller, vertical pipes which spray the sewage over the stones.

Another much-used method consists of a vertical pipe in the center of the filter connected to rotating horizontal pipes which spray the sewage continuously upon the stones.

The trend today is toward the use of the activated sludge process instead of trickling filters. This process speeds up the work of the bacteria by bringing air and sludge heavily laden with bacteria into close contact with the sewage.

After the sewage leaves the settling tank in primary treatment, it is pumped to an aeration tank where it is mixed with air and sludge loaded with bacteria and allowed to remain for several hours. During this time, the bacteria break down the organic matter.

From the aeration tank, the sewage, now called mixed liquor, flows to another sedimentation tank to remove the solids. Chlorination of the effluent completes the basic secondary treatment.

The sludge, now activated with additional millions of bacteria and other tiny organisms, can be used again by returning it to an aeration tank for mixing with new sewage and ample amounts of air.

The activated sludge process, like most other techniques, has advantages and limitations. The size of the units necessary for this treatment is small, thereby requiring less land space and the process is free of flies and odors. But it is more costly to operate than the filter, and the activated sludge process sometimes loses its effectiveness when faced with difficult industrial wastes.

An adequate supply of oxygen is necessary for the activated sludge process to be effective. Air is mixed with sewage and biologically active sludge in the aeration tanks by three different methods.

The first, mechanical aeration, is accomplished by drawing the sewage from the bottom of the tank and spraying it over the surface, thus causing the sewage to absorb large amounts of oxygen from the atmosphere.

In the second method, large amounts of air under pressure are piped down into the sewage and forced out through openings in the pipe. The third method is a combination of mechanical aeration and the force air method.

The final phase of the secondary treatment consists of the addition of chlorine, as the most common method of disinfection, to the effluent coming from the trickling filter or the activated sludge process. Chlorine is usually purchased in liquid form, converted to a gas, and injected into the effluent 15 to 30 minutes before the treated water is discharged into a watercourse. If done properly, Chlorination will kill more than 99 percent of the harmful bacteria in an effluent.

Lagoons and Septic Tanks

There are many well-populated areas in the United States that are not served by any sewer systems or waste treatment plants. Lagoons and septic tanks may act as less than satisfactory alternatives at such locations.

A septic tank is simply a tank buried in the ground to treat the sewage from an individual home. Waste water from the home flows into the tank where bacteria in the sewage may break down the organic matter and the cleaner water flows out of the tank into the ground through sub-surface drains. Periodically, the sludge or solid matter in the bottom of the tank must be removed and disposed of.

In a rural setting, with the right kind of soil and the proper location, the septic tank may be a reasonable and temporary means of disposing of strictly domestic wastes. Septic tanks should always be located so that none of the effluent can seep into sources used for drinking.

Lagoons, or, as they are sometimes called, stabilization or oxidation ponds, also have several advantages when used correctly.

They can give sewage primary and secondary treatment or they can be used to supplement other processes.

A lagoon is a scientifically constructed pond, usually three to five feet deep, in which sunlight, algae, and oxygen interact to restore water to a quality that is often equal to or better than effluent from secondary treatment. Changes in the weather may change the effectiveness of lagoons.

When used with other waste treatment processes, lagoons can be very effective. A good example of this is the Santee, California, water reclamation project. After conventional primary and secondary treatment by activated sludge, the town's waste water is kept in a lagoon for 30 days. Then the effluent, after chlorination, is pumped to land immediately above a series of lakes and allowed to trickle down through sandy soil into the lakes. The resulting water is of such good quality the residents of the area can swim, boat, and fish in the lake water.

THE NEED FOR FURTHER TREATMENT OF WASTES

In the past, pollution control was concerned primarily with problems caused by domestic and the simpler wastes of industry. Control was aimed principally towards protecting downstream public water supplies and stopping or preventing nuisance conditions.

Pollution problems were principally local in extent and their control a local matter.

This is no longer true. National growth and change have altered this picture. Progress in abating pollution has been outdistanced by population growth, the speed of industrial progress and technological developments, changing land practices, and many other factors.

The increased production of goods has greatly increased the amounts of common industrial wastes. New processes in manufacturing are producing new, complex wastes that sometimes defy present pollution control technology. The increased application of commercial fertilizers and the development and widespread use of a vast array of new pesticides are resulting in a host of new pollution problems from water draining off land.

The growth of the nuclear energy field and the use of radioactive materials foreshadow still another complicating and potentially serious water pollution situation.

Long stretches of both interstate and intrastate streams are subjected to pollution which ruins or reduces the use of the water for many purposes. Conventional biological waste treatment processes are hard-pressed to hold the pollution line, and for a growing number of our larger cities, these processes are no longer adequate.

Our growing population not only is packing our central cities but spreading out farther and farther into suburbia and exurbia. Across the country, new satellite communities are being born almost daily. The construction or extension of sewer lines has not matched either the growth rate or its movements. Sea water intrusion is a growing problem in coastal areas. It is usually caused by the excessive pumping of fresh water from the ground which lowers the water level, allowing salt water to flow into the ground water area.

The Types of Pollutants

Present-day problems that must be met by sewage treatment plants can be summed up in the eight types of pollutants affecting our waters.

The eight general categories are: common sewage and other oxygen-demanding wastes; disease-causing agents; plant nutrients; synthetic organic chemicals; inorganic chemicals and other mineral substances; sediment; radioactive substances; and heat.

Oxygen-demanding wastes — These are the traditional organic waste and ammonia contributed by domestic sewage and industrial wastes of plant and animal origin. Besides human sewage, such wastes result from food processing, paper mill production, tanning, and other manufacturing processes. These wastes are usually destroyed by bacteria if there is sufficient oxygen present in the water. Since fish and other aquatic life depend on oxygen for life, the oxygen-demanding wastes must be controlled, or the fish die.

Disease-causing agents — This category includes infectious organisms which are carried into surface and ground water by sewage from cities and institutions, and by certain kinds of industrial wastes, such as tanning and meat packing plants. Man or animals come in contact with these microbes either by drinking the water or through swimming, fishing, or other activities. Although modern disinfection techniques have greatly reduced the danger of this type of pollutant, the problem must be watched constantly.

Plant nutrients — These are the substances in the food chain of aquatic life, such as algae and water weeds, which support and stimulate their growth. Carbon, nitrogen, and phosphorus are the three chief nutrients present in natural water. Large amounts of these nutrients are produced by sewage, certain industrial wastes, and drainage from fertilized lands. Biological waste treatment processes do not remove the phosphorus and nitrogen to any substantial extent -- in fact, they convert the organic forms of these substances into mineral form, making them more usable by plant life. The problem starts when an excess of these nutrients over-stimulates the growth of water plants which cause unsightly conditions, interfere with treatment processes, and cause unpleasant and disagreeable tastes and odors in the water.

Synthetic organic chemicals — Included in this category are detergents and other household aids, all the new synthetic organic pesticides, synthetic industrial chemicals, and the wastes from their manufacture. Many of these substances are toxic to fish and aquatic life and possibly harmful to humans. They cause taste and odor problems and resist conventional waste treatment. Some are known to be highly poisonous at very low concentrations. What the long-term effects of small doses of toxic substances may be is not yet known.

Inorganic chemicals and mineral substances — A vast array of metal salts, acids, solid matter, and many other chemical compounds are included in this group. They reach our waters from mining and manufacturing processes, oil field operations, agricultural practices, and natural sources. Water used in irrigation picks up large amounts of minerals as it filters down through the soil on its way to the nearest stream. Acids of a wide variety are discharged as wastes by industry, but the largest single source of acid in our water comes from mining operations and mines that have been abandoned. Many of these types of chemicals are being created each year. They interfere with natural stream purification, destroy fish and other aquatic life, cause excessive hardness of water supplies, corrode expensive water treatment equipment, increase commercial and recreational boat maintenance costs, and boost the cost of waste treatment.

Sediments — These are the particles of soils, sands, and minerals washed from the land and paved areas of communities into the water. Construction projects are often large sediment producers. While not as insidious as some other types of pollution, sediments are a major problem because of the sheer magnitude of the amount reaching our waterways. Sediments fill stream channels and harbors, requiring expensive dredging, and they fill reservoirs, reducing their capacities and useful life. They erode power turbines and pumping equipment, and reduce fish and shellfish populations by blanketing fish nests and food supplies. More importantly, sediments reduce the amount of sunlight penetrating the water. The sunlight is required by green aquatic plants which produce the oxygen necessary to normal stream balance. Sediments greatly increase the treatment costs for municipal and industrial water supply and for sewage treatment where combined sewers are in use.

Radioactive substances — Radioactive pollution results from the mining and processing of radioactive ores; from the use of refined radioactive materials in power reactors and for industrial, medical, and research purposes; and from fallout following nuclear weapons testing. Increased use of these substances poses a potential public health problem. Since radiation accumulates in humans, control of this type of pollution must take into consideration total exposure in the human environment -- water, air, food, occupation, and medical treatment.

Heat — Heat reduces the capacity of water to absorb oxygen. Tremendous volumes of water are used by power plants and industry for cooling. Most of the water, with the added heat, is returned to streams, raising their temperatures. With less oxygen, the water is not as efficient in assimilating oxygen-consuming wastes and in supporting fish and aquatic life. Unchecked waste heat discharges can seriously alter the ecology of a lake, a stream, or even part of the sea.

Water in lakes or stored in impoundments can be greatly affected by heat. Summer temperatures heat up the surfaces, causing the water to form into layers, with the cooler water forming the deeper layers. Decomposing vegetative matter from natural and man-made pollutants deplete the oxygen from these cooler lower layers with harmful effects on the aquatic life. When the oxygen-deficient water is discharged from the lower gates of a dam, it may have serious effects on downstream fish life and reduce the ability of the stream to assimilate downstream pollution.

To complicate matters, most of our wastes are a mixture of the eight types of pollution, making the problems of treatment and control that much more difficult.

Municipal wastes usually contain oxygen-consuming pollutants, synthetic organic chemicals such as detergents, sediments, and other types of pollutants. The same is true of many industrial wastes which may contain, in addition, substantial amounts of heat from cooling processes. Water that drains off the land usually contains great amounts of organic matter in addition to sediment. Also, land drainage may contain radioactive substances and pollutants washed from the sky, vegetation, buildings, and streets during rainfall.

ADVANCED METHODS OF TREATING WASTES

These new problems of a modern society have placed additional burden upon our waste treatment systems. Today's pollutants are more difficult to remove from the water. And increased demands upon our water supply aggravate the problem. During the dry season, the flow of rivers decreases to such an extent that they have difficulty in assimilating the effluent from waste treatment plants.

In the future, these problems will be met through better and more complete methods of removing pollutants from water and better means for preventing some wastes from even reaching our streams in the first place.

The best immediate answer to these problems is the widespread application of existing waste treatment methods. Many cities that have only primary treatment need secondary treatment. Many other cities need enlarged or modernized primary and secondary systems.

But this is only a temporary solution. The discharge of oxygen-consuming wastes will increase despite the universal application of the most efficient waste treatment processes now available. And these are the simplest wastes to dispose of. Conventional treatment processes are already losing the battle against the modern-day, tougher wastes.

The increasing need to reuse water now calls for better and better waste treatment. Every use of water — whether in home, in the factory, or on the farm — results in some change in its quality.

To return water of more usable quality to receiving lakes and streams, new methods for removing pollutants are being developed. The advanced waste treatment techniques under investigation range from extensions of biological treatment capable of removing nitrogen and phosphorus nutrients to physical-chemical separation techniques such as adsorption, distillation, and reverse osmosis.

These new processes can achieve any degree of pollution control desired and, as waste effluents are purified to higher and higher degrees by such treatment, the point is reached where effluents become *too good to throw away.*

Such water can be deliberately and directly reused for agricultural, industrial, recreational, or even drinking water supplies. This complete water renovation will mean complete pollution control and, at the same time, more water for the nation.

Coagulation-Sedimentation

The application of advanced techniques for waste treatment, at least in the next several years, will most likely take up where primary and secondary treatment leave off. Ultimately, entirely new systems will no doubt replace the modern facilities of today.

The process known as coagulation-sedimentation may be used to increase the removal of solids from effluent after primary and secondary treatment. Besides removing essentially all of the settleable solids, this method can, with proper control and sufficient addition of chemicals, reduce the concentration of phosphate by over 95 percent.

In this process, alum, lime, or iron salts are added to effluent as it comes from the secondary treatment. The flow then passes through flocculation tanks where the chemicals cause the smaller particles to floc or bunch together into large masses.

The larger masses of particles or lumps will settle faster when the effluent reaches the next step — the sedimentation tank.

Although used for years in the treatment of industrial wastes and in water treatment, coagulation-sedimentation is classified as an advanced process because it is not usually applied to the treatment of municipal wastes. In many cases, the process is a necessary pre-treatment for some of the other advanced techniques.

Adsorption

Technology has also been developed to effect the removal of refractory organic materials. These materials are the stubborn organic matter which persists in water and resists normal biological treatment.

The effects of the organics are not completely understood, but taste and odor problems in water, tainting of fish flesh, foaming of water, and fish kills have been attributed to such materials.

Adsorption consists of passing the effluent through a bed of activated carbon granules which will remove more than 98 percent of the organics. To cut down the cost of the procedure, the carbon granules can be cleaned by heat and used again.

An alternative system utilizing powdered carbon is under study. Rather than pass the effluent through a bed of granules, the powdered carbon is put directly into the stream. The organics stick to the carbon, and then the carbon is removed from the effluent by using coagulating chemicals and allowing the coagulated carbon particles to settle in a tank.

The use of this finely ground carbon will improve the rate at which the refractory organics are removed. The potential widespread use of powdered carbon adsorption depends largely on the effectiveness of regenerating the carbon for use again.

Except for the salts added during the use of water, municipal waste water that has gone through the previous advanced processes will be restored to a chemical quality almost the same as before it was used.

When talking of salts in water, salt is not limited to the common kind that is used in the home for seasoning food. In waste treatment language, salts mean the many minerals dissolved by water as it passes through the air as rainfall, as it trickles through the soil and over rocks, and as it is used in the home and factory.

Electrodialysis

Electrodialysis is a rather complicated process by which electricity and membranes are used to remove salts from an effluent. A membrane is usually made of chemically treated plastic. The salts are forced out of the water by the action of an electric field. When a mineral salt is placed in water, it has a tendency to break down into ions. An ion is an atom or a small group of atoms having an electrical charge.

As an example, the two parts of common table salt are sodium and chlorine. When these two elements separate as salt dissolves in water, the sodium and chlorine particles are called ions. Sodium ions have a positive charge, while chlorine ions have a negative charge.

When the effluent passes through the electrodialysis cell, the positive sodium ions are attracted through a membrane to a pole or electrode that is negatively charged. The negatively charged chlorine ions are pulled out of the water through another membrane toward an electrode with a positive charge.

With the salts removed by the action of the two electrodes, the clean water flows out of the electrodialysis cell for reuse or discharge into a river or stream.

As a city uses its water, the amount of salts in the water increases by 300-400 milligrams per liter. Fortunately, electrodialysis can remove this buildup of salts.

In other words, this process returns the salt content of the water back to where it was or even better than when the city first received the water.

The Blending of Treated Water

Properly designed and applied, the methods that have been explained will be able to supply any quality of water for any reuse.

But none of these processes will stand alone. They must be used in a series or a parallel plan. In a series, all the sewage passes through all the processes, one after another, each process making a particular contribution toward improving the water. For example, the conventional primary treatment removes the material that will readily settle or float; the secondary biological step takes care of the decomposable impurities; coagulation-sedimentation, the third, step, eliminates the suspended solids; carbon adsorption removes the remaining dissolved organic matter; electrodialysis returns the level of the salts to what it was before the water was used; and, finally, chlorination provides the health safety barrier against disease carriers.

Basically, the same result can be achieved by separating the effluent into two streams. In this instance, all of the waste receives the primary and secondary treatment and then passes through the coagulation-sedimentation and adsorption processes which remove the organic matter. Half of the sewage is then treated by evaporation and adsorption to remove all impurities including the minerals. This effluent, when blended with the other half, can provide water with the desired level of minerals. After chlorination, the water can be reused.

Almost any degree of water quality can be achieved by varying the flow of the two streams. This technique reduces the treatment cost, since only a fraction of the flow requires treatment with the more expensive unit processes, such as distillation.

Distillation or evaporation basically consists of bringing the effluent to the boiling point. The steam or vapor produced is piped to another chamber where it is cooled, changing it back to a liquid. Most of the unwanted polluting impurities remain in the original chamber. However, some volatile substances may distill along with the water and carry along foreign materials that contribute objectionable taste.

As most people have discovered, distilled water has a flat, disagreeable taste caused by the absence of minerals and air. But by blending this pure water with water that still contains some minerals, a clean, better tasting water results. And, just as importantly, the more expensive distillation process is used on only part of the effluent, and the rest of the waste water is treated by the less costly procedures.

NEW CHALLENGES FOR WASTE TREATMENT

So far, the most readily available processes that will solve most current pollution problems have been covered. But the future holds many new challenges. Scientists are still looking for the ultimate system that will do the complete job of cleaning up water, simply and at a reasonable cost.

One such possible process under study is reverse osmosis. When liquids with different concentrations of mineral salts are separated by a membrane, molecules of pure water tend to pass by osmosis from the more concentrated to the less concentrated side until both liquids have the same mineral content.

Scientists are now exploring ways to take advantage of the natural phenomena of osmosis, but in reverse. When pressure is exerted on the side with the most minerals, this natural force reverses itself, causing the molecules of pure water to flow out of the compartment containing a high salt concentration.

This means that perfectly pure water is being taken out of the waste rather than taking pollutants out of water as is the traditional way. And this process takes clean water away from everything — bacteria, detergents, nitrates.

Tests have shown that the theory works well, resulting in water good enough to drink. Efforts are now under way to develop large membranes with long life. Also, the process and equipment need to be tested on a large scale.

Many other techniques to improve waste treatment are under development in laboratories and in the field.

For example, special microscopic organisms are being tested for removing nitrates from waste water by reducing the nitrates to elemental nitrogen.

Chemical Oxidation

Municipal waste waters contain many organic materials only partially removed by the conventional treatment methods. Oxidants such as ozone and chlorine have been used for many years to improve the taste and odor qualities or to disinfect municipal drinking water. They improve the quality of water by destroying or altering the structure of the chemicals in the water.

However, the concentration of the organic materials in drinking water supplies is much less than it is in the waste-bearing waters reaching treatment plants. Until recently, the cost of the oxidants has prevented the use of this process in the treating of wastes. Now improvements in the production and application of ozone and pure oxygen may reduce costs sufficiently to make their use practicable. When operated in conjunction with other processes, oxidation could become an effective weapon in eliminating wastes resistant to other processes.

<u>Polymers and Pollution</u>

In discussing the coagulation-sedimentation process, mention was made of the use of alum or lime to force suspended solids into larger masses. The clumping together helps speed up one of the key steps in waste treatment — the separation of solids and liquids.

During the past 25 years, the chemical industry has been working on synthetic organic chemicals, known as polyelectrolytes or polymers, to further improve the separation step.

Formerly, polymers have proved effective when used at a later stage of treatment -- the sludge disposal step. Sludge must be dewatered so that it can be more easily disposed of. By introducing polymers into the sludge, the physical and chemical bonds between the solids are tightened. When this happens, the water can be extracted more rapidly.

Wider use of polymers is now being investigated. By putting polymers into streams or rivers, it may be possible to capture silt at specified locations so that it can be removed in quantity.

If polymers are put into raw sewage, waste treatment plants may be able to combine a chemical process with the standard primary and secondary stages. And this method of removing solids can be applied immediately without lengthy and expensive addition of buildings or new facilities.

The chemicals also hold promise as a means of speeding the flow of waste waters through sewer systems, thus, in effect, increasing the capacity of existing systems.

THE PROBLEM OF WASTE DISPOSAL

No matter how good the treatment of wastes, there is always something left over. It may be the rags and sticks that were caught on the screens at the very beginning of the primary treatment. It could be brine or it could be sludge — that part of the sewage that settles to the bottom in sedimentation tanks. Whatever it is, there is always something that must be burned, buried, or disposed of in some manner.

It is a twofold problem. The sludge or other matter must be disposed of to complete a city's or industry's waste treatment. And it must be disposed of in a manner not to add to or upset the rest of the environment.

If it is burned, it must be done in a way not to add to the pollution of the atmosphere. This would only create an additional burden for our already overburdened air to cope with. And air pollutants by the action of rain and wind have a habit of returning to the water, complicating the waste treatment problem rather than helping it.

There are many methods and processes for dealing with the disposal problem, which is sometimes referred to as the problem of ultimate disposal. The most common method for disposing of sludge and other waste concentrates consists of digestion followed by filtration and incineration.

The digestion of sludge takes place in heated tanks where the material can decompose naturally and the odors can be controlled. As digested sludge consists of 90 to 95 percent water, the next step in disposal must be the removal of as much of the water as possible.

Water can be removed from sludge by use of a rotating filter drum and suction. As the drum rotates in the sludge, the water is pulled through the filter and the residues are peeled off for disposal. For more effective dewatering, the sludge can be first treated with a coagulant chemical such as lime or ferric chloride to produce larger solids before the sludge reaches the filter.

Drying beds which are usually made of layers of sand and gravel can be used to remove water from sludge. The sludge is spread over the bed and allowed to dry. After a week or two of drying, the residue will be reduced in volume and, consequently, will be easier to dispose.

Incineration consists of burning the dried sludge to reduce the residues to a safe, non-burnable ash. The ash can be disposed of by filling unused land or by dumping it well out into the ocean. Since most of the pollutants have been removed by the burning, the ash should cause very little change in the quality of the ocean waters.

A very promising new method of sludge disposal gets rid of the unwanted sludge and helps restore a ravaged countryside. In many areas of the country, tops of hills and mountains were sliced away to get at the coal beneath. This strip mining left ugly gashes and scars in otherwise beautiful valleys of many states. It would take nature many years to restore the denuded areas.

With the new disposal idea, digested sludge in semi-liquid form is piped to the spoiled areas. The slurry containing many nutrients from the wastes, is spread over the land to give nature a hand in returning grass, trees, and flowers to the barren hilltops.

Restoration of the countryside will also help in the control of acids that drain from mines into streams and rivers, endangering the fish and other aquatic life and adding to the difficulty in reusing the water. Acids are formed when pyrite containing iron and sulfur is exposed to the air.

Sludge or other waste concentrates are not always costly burdens. By drying and other processes, some cities have produced fertilizers that are sold to help pay for part of the cost of treating wastes. If not sold to the public, some municipalities use the soil enrichers on parks, road parkways, and other public areas.

Some industries have found they can reclaim certain chemicals during waste treatment and reuse them in manufacturing or refining processes. Other firms have developed saleable by-products from residues in waste treatment.

More studies are going on to find greater use for sludge to help solve the disposal problem and to help offset the cost of waste treatment.

CHEMISTRY

A knowledge of chemistry is desirable for all treatment processes , first to control the processes occurring in their plants and, second, to measure the effectiveness of such treatment as is used.

Chemistry, in its broad sense, deals with the composition of matter and how it changes. A description of matter should include a statement telling of what it is made and the manner or state in which it exists. Thus a description of water should state that it is composed of hydrogen and oxygen in certain proportions and exists as a liquid. Ice also is composed of hydrogen and oxygen in the same proportions, but exists as a solid. Such a change in matter is called a physical change and takes place when its manner or physical state of existence is changed but its chemical composition remains unaltered.

A *chemical change* is an alteration of the composition of matter, as that which takes place when quick lime is slaked to form hydrated lime or when iron rusts.

Actions or measurements relating to physical changes, such as temperature, rates of settling, particle size, velocity of flow, etc., are dealt with under the science of physics. Chemistry deals with the composition and change in composition of matter. It may be subdivided into two branches. Analytical chemistry deals with the breaking down of matter into its fundamental components. Synthetic chemistry is concerned with the building up of matter from its elemental constituents. Years of investigations have shown that all matter is composed of combinations of one or more fundamental substances called elements.

Elements are substances which cannot be subdivided into simpler sub-substances by ordinary chemical change. Water can be broken down into hydrogen and oxygen, but it has not been possible to break down hydrogen or oxygen to produce simpler substances. Therefore, hydrogen and oxygen are elements. In all, there are 102 stable elements, of which less than twenty are of importance to the chemistry of sewage treatment. A partial list of chemical elements is shown in Table 11. Elements themselves are made up of unit particles called atoms.

Atoms are the smallest pieces of an element that can take part in a chemical change. You might consider atoms as extremely small building blocks, each one of any single element being chemically the same, but different from atoms of other elements.

Isotopes are elements that may contain two or more distinct kinds of atoms, identical in their general chemical properties but differing essentially in mass. Most of the ordinary elements consist of mixtures of isotopes. Thus, chlorine consists of a mixture of two isotopes of mass 35 and of mass 37 in such proportion that the average atomic weight is 35.46.

TABLE 11

Basic Data for Elements and Radicals Encountered in Sewage Treatment (only the most common valences shown).

	Atomic Symbol	Atomic Weight	Valence	Combining Weight
Elements				
Aluminum	Al	26.98	+3	8.99
Calcium	Ca	40.08	+2	20.04
Carbon	C	12.01	+4	3.00
Chlorine	Cl	35.46	-1	35.46
Copper	Cu	63.54	+2	31.77
Hydrogen	H	1.008	+1	1.008
Iodine	I	126.91	-1	126.91
Iron	Fe	55.85	+3	18.62
Magnesium	Mg	24.32	+2	12.16
D	Mn	54.93	Several	
Manganese				
Nitrogen	N	14.01	Several	
Oxygen	O	16.00	-2	8.00
Potassium	K	39.10	+1	39.10
Sodium	Na	23.00	+1	23.00
Sulfur	S	32.06	Several	
Radicals				
Hydroxyl	(OH)		-1	17.00
Nitrite	(NO_2)		-1	46.01
Nitrate	$(NO,)$		1	62.01
Sulfate	$(SO_{4.})$		2	48.03
Carbonate	$(CO,)$		2	30.00
Bicarbonate	(HCO_3)		1	61.01
Phosphate	(PO_4)		3	31.66
Silicate	(SiO_3)		2	38.05
Ammonium	(NH_4)		+1	17.03

Atoms of an element may combine with each other or with atoms of other elements to form molecules. *Molecules* are the smallest portions of a substance that can exist and still retain the composition of the substance. If two atoms of chlorine combine, we have a molecule of chlorine gas, which is how the free element chlorine exists in nature. If one atom of chlorine combines with one atom of sodium, a molecule of ordinary table salt is produced. When atoms of different elements combine, the product is called a compound and the smallest piece of a compound that can exist and retain the composition of the compound is a molecule. If we again consider atoms as building blocks and the blocks cannot be subdivided, it must follow that atoms of elements combine with atoms of other elements in steps of one atom at a time. Thus, one, two or three atoms of one element can combine with one, two or three atoms of another element, but never with a fraction of an atom.

Law of multiple proportions. This idea that matter is composed of combination of blocks, called atoms, explains the fact that elements can only combine with each other in certain definite proportions or multiples thereof. This immediately brings some order out of what might be chaos. One atom of carbon will combine with one atom of oxygen to form carbon monoxide. If one atom of carbon united with two atoms of oxygen, the product would not be the same. Actually, when one atom of carbon combines with two atoms of oxygen, an entirely different compound called carbon dioxide is formed. If we think of compounds as consisting of an aggregate of molecules each of which is made up of a definite proportion of atoms of different elements, then we can understand why a pure compound is always exactly the same in composition, regardless of how it is made or where it is found. Water, made by exploding hydrogen and oxygen, always is one part hydrogen by weight, and eight parts oxygen. Water made from burning gasoline is exactly the same. Water in Timbuktu, and water in the jelly you eat is all composed of one part hydrogen and eight parts oxygen by weight.

Atoms are extremely small particles which cannot be isolated and weighed. However, the weights of atoms of different elements can be compared and a relative weight obtained for each. As oxygen combines with many elements, it is convenient to consider it as a sort of standard for weight comparison and further, if a weight value of 16 is assigned to oxygen no element will have a combining weight less than one.

As molecules are composed of atoms, it must follow that the weight of a molecule is the sum of the weights of each atom that makes up the molecule.

Molecular weight is the sum of the atomic weights of the elements in the molecule. Thus, water is composed of 2 atoms of hydrogen, each of atomic weight 1.0 and one atom of oxygen, atomic weight 16, making the molecular weight of water 2 X 1 + 16 = 18. Similarly, carbon dioxide is one carbon atom 12, and two oxygen atoms each 16, making the molecular weight 12 + 2 X 16 = 44.

Names-The names of elements have been generally derived from Creek and Latin roots descriptive of their character. Thus, iodine is named from its violet color, chlorine from its green color, others from localities where they were discovered, and others are derived from the names of minerals from which they were extracted.

When only 'wo elements unite to form a compound, the name of the second element is modified to end in *ide*. Thus, when sodium and chlorine are combined to form a salt, it is called sodium chloride. Compounds of one element with oxygen are called oxides and when more than one oxygen atom is present, the Greek prefix *di* for two and *tri* for three is added. Thus, sulfur dioxide arid sulfur trioxide describe sulfur compounds containing two or three atoms of oxygen for each atom of sulfur.

Symbols. To illustrate chemical changes, symbols have been developed for the different elements which indicate one atom of the element. Thus, an atom of chlorine may be written as Cl and of oxygen as 0. Generally, the symbol is the first or first and second letter of the name of the element, although often the English name of the element is given but the abbreviation of the Latin or Greek name is used as the symbol. Thus, sodium is Na, the abbreviation of natrium, and iron is Fe, the abbreviation of ferrum. These symbols, together with the names of the common elements, are given in Table 10.

Formulae. By use of these symbols it is possible to write formulae which indicate the number and kinds of atoms making up a molecule. For example, HCl means that a molecule of hydrochloric acid is composed of one atom of hydrogen and one atom of chlorine. When more than one atom of an element occurs in a molecule, it is indicated by a number written under the symbol. Thus, H_2SO_4 means that a molecule of sulfuric acid contains two atoms of hydrogen, one of sulfur and four of oxygen. When a group of atoms is enclosed in parenthesis and a subscript number used, it means the whole group occurs in the moleule as many times as the value of the subscript numbers. For example: $Fe2(SO_4)_3$ means iron sulfate contains two atoms of iron and three sulfate groups each containing one atom of sulfur and four atoms of oxygen. This is done because certain elements combine to form groups which react with other elements in a manner similar to a single element. The group is called a radical and will be discussed more fully under solutions. See Table 10. Another type of group symbol is used to indicate the association of molecules of complex compounds with molecules of simpler compounds. The latter can enter into or be expelled from the complex molecule without themselves being changed. For example, aluminum sulfate is $Al_2(SO_4)_3$ but if prepared by cyrstallization from a water solution it will retain molecules of water and have the formula $Al_2(SO_4)_3 \cdot 18H_2O$, which is chemically like filter alum. This means that for every molecule of $Al_2(SO_4)_3$ present in the compound there are also eighteen molecules of water. However, if the compound is heated, the water as such can be expelled from the compound. Formulae of common chemicals with their common and chemical name are given in *Table 12* below.

Equations. By use of these formulae it is possible to write chemical changes graphically.

Thus, $CaCO_3 + H_2SO_4 \rightarrow CaSO_4 + H_2CO_3$ means that when calcium carbonate and sulfuric acid react or combine, calcium sulfate and carbonic acid are formed. Similarly, when iron

rusts it combines with oxygen to form iron oxide. This can be written $Fe + 3 O_2 \rightarrow 2Fe_2O_3$ However, one of the laws of chemistry is that matter can neither be created nor destroyed. Hence, in any chemical change there must be the same number of atoms in the substances produced as were present in the original compounds. Therefore, the above reaction must be "balanced" to produce an "equation" having an equal number of atoms on each side of the equation. Iron oxide, the product of the above reaction, contains two atoms of iron and three atoms of oxygen. To balance the equation there must be the same number of atoms of iron and oxygen reacting as exists in the product, Fe_2O_3. We might try to write the equation

$2Fe + 3O \rightarrow Fe_2O_3$, but this cannot be true because we know oxygen gas consists of two atoms or O_2. To make the equation conform to the facts, we then multiply everything by two.

Thus, $4Fe + 3 O_2 \rightarrow 2Fe_2O_3$, Now we have said that four atoms of iron react with three molecules of oxygen gas to produce two molecules of iron oxide, and the number of atoms on each side of the equation are equal.

TABLE 12

Common Name	Chemical Name	Formula
Ammonia gas...	Ammonia	NH_3
Ammonia	Ammonium hydroxide	NH_4OH
Filter alum	Aluminum sulfate	$Al_2(SO_4)_3.14H_2O$
Limestone	Calcium carbonate	$CaCO_3$
	Calcium bicarbonate	$Ca(HCO_3)_2$
Hydrated lime	Calcium hydroxide	$Ca(OH)_2$
Quick lime	Calcium oxide	CaO
	Chlorine	Cl_2
	Chlorine dioxide	ClO_2
Blue vitriol	Cupric sulfate	$CuSO_4.5H_2O$
	Ferric chloride	$FeCl_3.6H_2O$
Muriatic acid	Hydrochloric acid	HCl
	Sulfuric acid	H_2SO_4
Salt	Sodium chloride	$NaCl$
Soda ash	Sodium carbonate	Na_2CO_3
Soda	Sodium bicarbonate	$NaHCO_3$
Lye	Sodium hydroxide	$NaOH$
	Sodium phosphate	$Na_3PO_4.12H_2O$
	Water	H_2O
	Hypochlorous acid	$HOCl$
Chloride of lime	Calcium oxychloride	$CaOC_2$
	Aluminum hydroxide	$Al(OH)_3$
Gypsum	Calcium sulfate	$CaSO_4$
	Carbon dioxide	CO_2
	Carbonic acid	H_2CO_3
	Monochloramine	NH_2Cl
	Dichloramine	$NHCl_2$
	Nitrogen trichloride	NO_3
	Methane	CH_4
	Calcium hypochlorite	$Ca(OCl)_2$

From Table 11 we find the atomic weight of iron is 55.85 and of oxygen is 16.0. Then, 4 atoms of iron are equivalent to 4 X 55.85 = 223.40. A molecule of oxygen equals two atoms or 2 X 16.0 = 32.0, the molecular weight. Three molecules equal 3 X 32.0 = 96.0. A molecule of iron oxide equals 2 X 55.85 = 111.70. the weight of two atoms of iron, plus 3 X 16.0 = 48.0, the weight of three atoms of oxygen, or a total of 159.70. Two molecules of iron oxide = 2 X 159.70 or 319.40.

The calculations would be:

$$4Fe + 3O_2 = 2Fe_2O_3$$
$$4 \times 55.85 + 6 \times 16.0 = 319.40$$

Now we can say that 223.40 parts of iron react with 96.0 parts of oxygen to produce 319.40 parts of iron rust, and they always will do so because the law of multiple proportion states that elements combine only in definite proportions. Suppose we had a piece of iron that had rusted and we wanted to know how much iron had been lost. If we carefully gathered and weighed all the rust and found it to be 79.84 grams, then we can calculate by proportion that 79.84 : 319.40 = ? : 223.40, so the weight of iron that rusted must have been

$$\frac{79.84 \times 223.40}{319.40} = 55.84\text{grams}$$

To illustrate how this is of value to a sewage treatment plant operator, let's suppose you wanted to know how much alkalinity was in the sewage you had to treat. It might be for control of a chemical precipitation processor possibly in connection with corrosion control. Suppose you have available a solution of sulfuric acid containing 2 mg H_2SO_4 in each ml. By titration, which will be explained in the laboratory, you find that 5.6 ml of the acid neutralizes all the alkalinity in a 100-ml sample of water. Calling alkalinity $CaCO_3$. the equation is H_2SO_4 + $CaCO_3$ $CaSO_4$ + H_2CO_3. From the atomic weights, we find that 98 parts of sulfuric acid react with 100 parts of calcium carbonate. We found that 5.6 ml of a solution of sulfuric acid containing 2 mg per ml reacted with the alkalinity in the sample. Thus, by proportions,

$$\frac{5.6 \times 2}{98} = \frac{X}{100} \text{ and we find } X = 11.5\text{mgCaCO}_3$$

Therefore, this weight of calcium carbonate must have been present in the 100 ml of sample. If we wish to express the concentration as parts per million, the answer would be 10 X 11.5 or 115 mg per liter of sample, which is equal to 115 ppm. Actually, in doing the test, the concentration of acid is adjusted so that the titration in ml multiplied by 10, if a 100-ml sample is used, gives the answer directly without any calculation.

Equations commonly used in water and sewage treatment are:

$$CH_4 + 2_2 \rightarrow CO_2 + 2H_2O$$
$$Cl_2 + H_2O \rightleftharpoons HCl + HOCl$$
$$Ca(OCl)_2 + Na_2CO_3 \rightleftharpoons 2NaOCl + CaCO_3$$
$$Al_2(SO_4)_3 + 3CaCO_3 + 3H_2O \rightleftharpoons 2Al(OH)_3 + 3CaSO_4 + 3CO_2$$
$$CO_2 + H_2O \rightleftharpoons H_2CO_3$$
$$CaCO3 + H_2CO_3 \rightleftharpoons Ca(HCO_3)_2$$
$$Ca(HCO_3)_2 + Ca(OH)_2 \rightleftharpoons 2CaCO_3 + 2H_2O$$
$$Ca(HCO_3)_2 + Na_2CO_3 \rightleftharpoons CaCO_3 + 2NaHCO_3$$
$$NH_3 + HOCl \rightleftharpoons NH_2Cl + H_2O$$
$$NH_2Cl + HOCl \rightleftharpoons NHCl_2 + H_2O$$
$$NHCl_2 + HOCl \rightleftharpoons NCl_3 + H_2O$$
$$CaCO_3 + H_2SO_4 \rightleftharpoons CaSO_4 + H_2CO_3$$
$$Ca(HCO_3)_2 + H_2SO_4 \rightleftharpoons CaSO_4 + 2H_2CO_3$$

Ionization. Somewhat different conditions prevail when chemicals are dissolved in water. You might consider that molecules of water enter between the atoms making up the molecules of the chemicals. The force that holds the atoms together is electrical. If they are separated by the molecules of water, each atom has an electrical charge. This splitting of the molecules, when dissolved in water, into charged atoms is called ionization. The charged atoms are called ions. Sodium chloride, when dissolved, ionizes into sodium ions and chloride ions.

$$NaCl \rightarrow Na^+ + Cl^-$$

The ions must he of equal and opposite charge or else the solution itself would have a charge, which is not true. When a salt such as ferric chloride ionizes, the ferric ion must have three positive charges to offset the negative charges of the three chlorine atoms.

$$FeCl_3 \rightarrow Fe^{+++} + 3Cl^-$$

Radicals. Under the heading Formulae, groups of atoms called radicals were discussed and it was said the groups reacted similarly to single elements. What was meant was that salts of the radicals ionize to form charged radicals instead of splitting into their component atoms. Thus, sodium sulfate ionizes to form sodium ions and sulfate ions and not charged sulfur or oxygen atoms.

$$Na_2SO_4 \rightarrow 2Na+ + SO_4$$
$$Fe_2(SO_4)^3 \rightleftarrows 2Fe^{+++} + 3SO_4^-$$

Not all compounds ionize to the same degree. Some in dilute solutions are very nearly completely changed to ions, others are so little ionized that for practical purposes they may be considered un-ionized. Others vary anywhere between the two extremes. Actually, the ionization of salts is a reversible reaction and at equilibrium, which is rapidly established, as many molecules of a salt ionize as ions combine to form molecules. The reaction then should be written.

$$Fe_2(SO_4)^3 \rightleftarrows 2FE^{+++} + 3(SO_4)-$$

to indicate it is proceeding in both directions at the same time and at the same speed. It is well known that similar electrical charges repel each other and opposite charges attract each other. This explains why not all elements will react. If the electrical charges on the atoms are the same, no chemical reaction will take place. If the charges on the atoms are different, then combinations can generally be made to take place.

Acids. One of the characteristics of an acid is that it will ionize in water to produce positively charged hydrogen ions.

$$HCl \rightleftarrows H^+ + Cl^-$$

Not all acids ionize to the same degree. In dilute solution the "strong" acids such as hydrochloric, sulfuric and nitric acids ionize practically completely. This is why they are called "strong" acids, as the activity of an acid is determined by the degree of ionization. "Weak" acids only partially ionize. Thus, an equal amount of a "weak" acid would produce only a fraction of the amount of hydrogen ion that a "strong"" acid under similar conditions would produce.

Acids are also classified according to the number of hydrogen ions produced by one molecule of the acid.

$$\text{Example: Monoacid -HCl} \rightleftarrows H+ + Cl^-$$
$$\text{Diacid} - H_2SO_4 \rightleftarrows 2H+ + SO_4^-$$
$$\text{Triacid -}H_3PO_4 \rightleftarrows 3H+ + PO^-$$

Bases or alkalis are compounds which ionize in water to furnish hydroxyl ions (OH-). As with acids, bases ionize to different degrees.

"Strong" bases such as sodium hydroxide, and calcium hydroxide ionize to a high degree while "weak" bases only partially ionize.

Similar to acids, they are classified depending on whether one, two or three hydroxyl ions are produced by one molecule of base.

$$\text{Example:} \quad \text{Monobasic -NaOH} \rightleftarrows OH^- + Na^+$$

$$\text{Diabasic -Ca(OH)}_2 \rightleftarrows 2OH^- + Ca^{++}$$

$$\text{Tribasic -Al (OH)}_3 \rightleftarrows 3OH^- + Al^{+++}$$

Equivalents. An equivalent weight of an acid is that weight of an acid which will furnish one molecular weight in grams of hydrogen ion. For monoacids, it equals the molecular weight of the acid in grams, for diacids it is half the molecular weight in grams, for triacids it is one-third of the molecular weight in grams.

Similarly, an equivalent of a base in the molecular weight in grams that will furnish one molecular weight of hydroxyl ions (17 grams). It is equal to the molecular weight divided by the number of hydroxyl radicals per molecule.

An equivalent weight of a salt is the molecular weight divided by the number of charges on the ions produced in solution.

pH value. Water ionizes to a slight degree to produce both hydrogen ion and hydroxyl ion.

$$H_2O \rightleftarrows H^+ + OH^-$$

Thus, water might be considered both an acid and a base. Actually, because the concentration of both ions is the same, it is considered neutral. The concentration of both (H^+) and (OH-) in pure water is 0.0000001 expressed in terms of gram ions per liter. Rather than use decimal figures for measuring hydrogen ion concentration, a pH scale has been adopted to record concentration in whole numbers.

The following has been prepared in which the concentration of hydrogen ions is expressed in values which are decimal multiples of ten.

Ionic concentration as Grams oj
Hydrogen Ions (H^+) per Liter

of Solution		pH Value
1.0		0
0.1		1
0.01		2
0.001		3
0.0001		4
0.00001		5
0.000001		6
0.0000001	neutral	7
0.00000001		8
0.000000001		9
0.0000000001		10
0.00000000001		11
0.000000000001		12
0.0000000000001		13
0.00000000000001		14

The pH value is the number of places after the decimal point in the expression for the concentration of hydrogen ions per liter. It will be

noticed that as the concentration of hydrogen ion decreases the pH value in the opposite column increases.

For reasons beyond the scope of this discussion, the number of (H$^+$) ions multiplied by the number of (OH$^-$) ions always gives the same value. That is. if the number of (H$^+$) ions is increased ten fold, then the number of (OH$^-$) ions will be automatically reduced to one tenth of what they were before.

$$(H^+) \times (OH^-) = k \text{ (a constant value)}$$

Because of this relationship, a scale of p(OH) values could be prepared in which the p(OH) value would always be that number which when added to the pH value would equal 14. That is. a solution having a pH of 3.0 would have a p(OH) of 11 and a pH of 9.0 would correspond to a p(OH) of 5.0. Because of this fact, a measurement of pH is also, indirectly, a measure of the OH" ion concentration and a second scale is therefore not necessary. pH values greater than 7.0 indicate alkaline characteristics.

Returning to the idea of "strong" and "weak" acids, if "strong" acids are highly ionized and produce a high concentration of hydrogen ion, then the pH value will be low. If an equivalent amount of "weak" acid produces less hydrogen ion, then the pH will be below 7.0 but not as low as in the "strong" acid solution.

Neutralization of acids and bases. Consider what happens when an acid solution and alkaline solution, each containing one equivalent of acid and base, are mixed:

$$HCl \rightleftarrows H^+ + Cl^-$$
$$NaOH \rightleftarrows OH^- + Na^+$$

The resulting solution would contain one equivalent of H$^+$, one equivalent of OH$^-$, plus the Na+ and Cl-. It was stated that water ionizes to H+ and OH- and their concentration from water is only 0.0000001 equivalents per liter. Thus, in the mixed solution the H$^+$ and OH$^-$ would combine to produce water until the concentration of each was reduced from one equivalent of each to 0.0000001 equivalent of each.

$$H^+ + OH^- \rightleftarrows H_2O$$

In solution there would be left the Na^{++} Cl$^-$, which is what is obtained when NaCl is dissolved.

$$NaCl \rightleftarrows Na^+ + Cl^-$$

Both the acid and base would have disappeared. This mutual reaction of acids and bases is called neutralization. One equivalent of any acid will exactly neutralize one equivalent of any base with the production of a salt and water.

This is the basis of the determination of alkalinity in water. Under "Equations" it was shown how the alkalinity could be calculated if a solution containing a known amount of acid was used. However, if the acid solution is adjusted so that it contains a definite number of equivalents of acid, then one volume of the acid will neutralize an equal number of equivalents of base and no calculation is necessary.

Normal solution is one which contains one equivalent of acid or base per liter. Hence, equal volume of normal acids and bases exactly neutralize each other, or, if the acid is twice the normality of the base, half the volume will be required to neutralize one volume of base, ml X normality of acid = ml X normality of base

To determine alkalinity, a 1/50 normal acid solution is used to neutralize the alkalinity in 100 ml of sewage. If 5.6 ml of acid was required, then 5.6 (the ml of acid) multiplied by 1/50 (the normality of the acid) divided by 100 (the volume of the sample of sewage equals the normality of the sewage).

$$\frac{5.6 \times 0.02}{100} = \text{N of the sewage}$$

A normal solution of alkalinity equals the molecular weight of CaCO3 divided by 2 or 50 grams per liter. If the normality of the sewage as determined is multiplied by 50, the concentration of $CaCO_3$ in the sewage would be found in grams per liter. But the result desired is milligrams per liter, so that the grams per liter are multiplied by 1000 to change them into milligrams per liter or parts per million.

$$\frac{5.6 \times .02}{100} \times 50 \times 1000 = 56\text{ppm}$$

It will be noticed that all the factors cancel, leaving the answer obtained by multiplying the milliliter of acid used by 10, if 100 ml sample is used, or 20 if a 50 ml sample is used. Thus, to actually do the test all that is necessary is to titrate 100 ml sample of sewage, measure the volume of acid used in milliliters and multiply this volume by ten to obtain the alkalinity in parts per million.

Acidity, alkalinity and pH. Acidity of water is a measure of the *total* amount of acid substances (H+) present in water expressed as parts per million of equivalent calcium carbonate. It has been shown that one equivalent of .an acid (H+) equals one equivalent of a base (OH-). Therefore, it makes no difference whether the result is expressed as acid or base and for convenience acidity is reported as equivalnt of $CaCO_3$ because many times it is not known just what acids are present.

Alkalinity is a measure of the *total* amount of alkaline substances present in water and is expressed as parts per million of equivalent $CaCO_3$. Again this is done because the alkalis present might not be known but at least they are equivalent to the amount of $CaCO_3$ reported.

The activity of an acid or alkali is measured by the pH value. Thus, the more active the acid characteristics the lower will be the pH, or the more active the alkalis, the higher the pH will be. Alkalinity and pH are not the same, neither can be calculated from the other.

This can be illustrated as follows. If 1/1000 equivalent of a strong acid is added to 1 liter of water it will produce 1/1000 equivalent of H+. From the table on page 13 it is shown that 0.001 equivalents of H+ per liter equals pH 3.0. If 1/1000 equivalents of a weak acid, 10% ionized, is added to one liter of water, it will produce only one-tenth as much H+ or 0.001 X .1 = 0.0001 equivalents of H+ per liter and thus have a pH of 4.0. In both solutions the acidity or total amount of acid is the same, but one has a pH of 3.0 and the other 4.0. The one with the lower pH would more actively corrode iron than the one with the higher pH.

Organic Chemistry. The discussion so far has been concerned only with those compounds of mineral origin. There is another vast field of chemistry concerned with compounds of living matter or substances that had once been living matter. These are composed mainly of carbon, hydrogen and oxygen in many different proportions such as sugar, cellulose, or gasoline. Most of them do not ionize in water. Some, such as proteins, contain small amounts of nitrogen, sulfur and phosphorous. One characteristic of such compounds is that they volatilize on heating or burning, leaving no ash. The vegetable extract in natural water that causes the light yellow color similar to dilute tea is an organic compound. Algae, both dead and alive, are organic in nature, as is phenol, all of which cause taste and odor in water even in concentrations of only a few parts per billion instead of parts per million.

Most of the solid material suspended in sewage and a substantial part of the dissolved matter also is organic in nature. In fact sewage treatment is essentially a process for decomposing organic material into simpler chemical substances rapidly and under controlled conditions.

Solutions, Colloids and Suspensions. If small quantities of such common substances as salt, sugar or baking soda are added to water, the substances will disappear and the water will be just as clear as it was originally. Such a combination is called a solution and no chemical reaction has taken place between the dissolved substance, called the solute, and the dissolving liquid, called the solvent. The mixture may be thought of as molecules of the solute uniformly dispersed throughout the solvent such that there is no apparent interference with the passage of light through the solution.

On the other hand, if soil is mixed with water it will not disappear, but will prevent the passage of light through the water in proportion to the amount of the soil present. Such a mixture may be called a suspension and the permanency of the suspension is dependent on the coarseness and settleability of the soil particles.

If the soil contains very fine material, such as certain clays, some of it will remain uniformly dispersed throughout the water, but will still be visible and will diffuse a beam of light as it shines through. Such a mixture may be called a colloid or, as sometimes designated, a colloidal suspension.

The three terms, suspensions, colloids and solutions are thus used to differentiate progressively finer degrees of dispersion of substances in a liquid. The limit of the zones to which these terms apply is somewhat indefinite, arbitrary and beyond the scope of this chapter.

Colloidal suspensions are commonly found in sewage treatment. Raw sewage. Iinhoff tank effluent, the supernatant liquor from sludge digestion tanks all exhibit more or less turbidity which is colloidal in nature. The purification effected by trickling filter units is due in part to removal of colloidal material from the sewage by the jelly-like coating on the surface of the filter stones.

The Chemistry of Sewage Organic Matter. Most of the organic matter in domestic sewage consists of food scraps, fecal and urinary wastes from human bodies, vegetable matter, mineral and organic salts, and miscellaneous materials such as soap, synthetic detergents, etc. Some of these are solids, some are in solution, and some may be in colloidal suspension.

The food scraps are largely carbohydrates, proteins or fats. Fecal matter is made up of bits of undigested food, intestinal bacteria, and cellular waste from the body. Chemically it is probably largely body protein with some fats and considerable carbohydrates. The urinary wastes contain most of the nitrogen which is not retained in the body. This is in the form of ammonia or urea. Urea is a chemical compound which is easily decomposed to yield ammonia and carbon dioxide.

The vegetable matter in sewage is essentially garbage derived from kitchens of the community. Soaps, synthetic detergents, and mineral salts are, of course, waste products from domestic activities involving dish washing and laundering.

Saprophytic bacteria, always present in sewage, will decompose sewage organic matter, reducing the complex proteins, fats, and carbohydrates to simpler substances with production of simple gases such as carbon dioxide, hydrogen sulfide, methane, and ammonia and more complex substances such as organic acids, alcohols, etc. The course of the digestion and the resultant products are dependent to a large extent on the availability of oxygen. The products of digestion of sewage solids when oxygen is absent are quite different than the products of the digestion of the same material when oxygen is available. Digestion in the absence of free oxygen is called anaerobic digestion while that in the presence of free oxygen is called aerobic digestion.

Anaerobic digestion of sewage solids. The first stage of the digestion is characterized by the production of organic acids. Proteins, carbohydrates, and fats are decomposed by the anaerobic bacteria and the products of the decomposition are organic acids. This digestion stage is evident in sludge by a lowering of the pH and the presence of a disagreeable sour odor. Unless the amount of acid produced is excessive, the digestion will normally proceed to the second stage. With excess acidity, such as is obtained when the addition of fresh solids is too rapid, the bacteria will be destroyed and the process will end with the first stage.

The second stage is characterized by liquefaction of sewage solids under mildly acid conditions. The bacteria, by enzyme action, convert the insoluble solids material to the soluble form. This is in accordance with the requirements of the bacterial cells that all food material must be in solution before it can pass through the cell wall.

The third stage of digestion is characterized by production of gases. carbon dioxide, methane, and hydrogen sulfide; as well as an increase of pH and the production of carbonate salts.

The operator of a sewage plant can exert considerable control over the digestion process by taking steps to favor the orderly progression from one stage to another. In a properly operated sludge digestion tank, all three stages of digestion are progressing simultaneously but in different zones or layers within the tank. Physical and chemical tests for pH, the volume and identification of the gases produced, the relative amount of volatile material in the sludge solids and the drainability of the sludge when put on drying beds or on vacuum filters will reveal how well the process is going.

Aerobic digestion. In the aerobic digestion of sewage organic matter such as occurs in streams where the organic load is not excessive or on trickling filter units, the decomposition of the proteins, carbohydrates, and fats proceeds without the production of foul smelling organic acids and gases. The saprophytic bacteria have ample free oxygen available with which to accomplish the chemical transformations involved in decomposition of the complex compounds and the fixation of carbon, hydrogen, phosphorous, and sulfur elements into simple gases, relatively inert humus-like material, and mineral salts. Sewage plant operators are familiar with aerobic digestion which takes place in trickling filter units. The saprophytic bacteria are embedded in the gelatinous growth coating the stones, and humus material produced by the digestion periodically "unloads" from the filter and appears in the effluent.

The activated sludge process is another example of aerobic digestion of sewage organic matter. In this instance the consumption of free oxygen by the filamentous bacteria which are incorporated in the activated sludge is so rapid that extraordinary volumes of air are supplied by air compressors.